To my family and loved ones who helped to make this book possible through their continued encouragement and love. A special dedication to my wife Barbara, who is faithful in her walk with the Lord, a true blessing to our entire family.

Bigelow's
Virus Troubleshooting
Pocket Reference

Bigelow's
Virus
Troubleshooting
Pocket Reference

Ken Dunham

McGraw-Hill

New York   San Francisco   Washington, D.C.   Auckland   Bogotá
Caracas   Lisbon   London   Madrid   Mexico City   Milan
Montreal   New Delhi   San Juan   Singapore
Sydney   Tokyo   Toronto

McGraw-Hill

A Division of The McGraw-Hill Companies

4 5 6 7 8 9 0   DOC/DOC   0 5 4 3 2

ISBN 0-07-212627-2

The sponsoring editor for this book was Michael Sprague, the editing supervisor was Penny Linskey, and the production supervisor was Claire Stanley. It was set in Century Schoolbook by Don Feldman of McGraw-Hill's Professional Book Group composition unit, in cooperation with Spring Point Publishing Services.

Printed and bound by R. R. Donnelley & Sons Company.

Disclaimer and Cautions

It is *important* that you read and understand the following information. Please read it carefully!

PERSONAL RISK AND LIMITS OF LIABILITY

The repair of personal computers and their peripherals involves some amount of personal risk. Use *extreme* caution when working with ac and high-voltage power sources. Every reasonable effort has been made to identify and reduce areas of personal risk. You are instructed to read this book carefully *before* attempting the procedures discussed. If you are uncomfortable following the procedures that are outlined in this book, do *not* attempt them—refer your service to qualified service personnel.

NEITHER THE AUTHOR, THE PUBLISHER, NOR ANYONE DIRECTLY OR INDIRECTLY CONNECTED WITH THE PUBLICATION OF THIS BOOK SHALL MAKE ANY WARRANTY EITHER EXPRESSED OR IMPLIED, WITH REGARD TO THIS MATERIAL, INCLUDING, BUT NOT LIMITED TO, THE IMPLIED WARRANTIES OF QUALITY, MERCHANTABILITY, AND FITNESS FOR ANY PARTICULAR PURPOSE. Further, neither the author, publisher, nor anyone directly or indirectly connected with the publication of this book shall be liable for errors or omissions contained herein, or for incidental or consequential damages, injuries, or financial or material losses resulting from the use, or inability to use, the material contained herein. This material is provided AS IS, and the reader bears all responsibilities and risks connected with its use.

Contents

Preface

This handy, pocket-sized reference covers all the essential information needed to prevent, identify, and recover from virus and other malware infections. Sections are organized for quick referencing, making it easy for you to find just what you're looking for when you want to find something fast.

This book is designed for all levels of antivirus expertise. Inside this book you'll find comprehensive, yet concise, coverage of all the major areas of antivirus protection and troubleshooting:

- Macintosh and PC antivirus, including a table of all Macintosh system viruses to date

- Home, school, and corporate considerations

- Preventive measures, including a myriad of computing techniques, suggested policy, procedure, and contracts

- How to identify a hoax, along with a table of common hoaxes In the Wild today

- Detailed analysis of third party reviews as to which antivirus programs are consistently the best antivirus tool

- Detection and removal tips and tricks, covering a wide range of topics for both PC and Macintosh computers

- Advanced troubleshooting and recovery methods
- Large collection of valuable Internet antivirus links, including download sites and major vendors of antivirus software

KEN DUNHAM

Acknowledgments

Special thanks to Jacqueline Landman Gay, David A. Harley, Mikko Hypponen, Mary Landesman, and Rob Rosenberger for all of their hard work as technical reviewers of this book. Each member of the review team helped to improve the quality and value of this book for individuals working to protect computers against malware infections.

I would also like to thank all of the individuals who, over the years, have supported my growth into my profession, especially my friends at About.com. Your continued feedback, support, and motivation encourage me both personally and professionally.

Introduction

John works diligently into the night to complete his thesis, which is due early the next day. He makes considerable progress until midnight. Immediately after 12 A.M. his computer stops working. He restarts the computer, only to find that there is no longer an operating system on the hard drive! After hours of anxiety and troubleshooting the issue, John finds out that the entire contents of the hard drive, including his thesis, have been deleted by a virus. Unfortunately, John does not have a backup copy of his thesis on a disk. As he sits in despair, John wonders why this happened to him. He wonders what he could have done differently to avoid this tragic event.

Current Threat of Viruses

In generic terms, a virus is a computer program that is designed to replicate. Some viruses are very dangerous, deleting files on a disk, while others may only spread throughout an infected system. Similar threats, but technically different from viruses, include worms and Trojans. See Section 2 for a more detailed and technical definition of viruses and other malware.

At the time of writing this book, an estimated 5 to 10 new viruses are discovered daily, and this number is increasing over time. That's a current average of over 200 new viruses each month. Roughly 20 of these new viruses are designed to wreak havoc on a system, executing a malicious payload. The remaining 180 viruses may not be as malicious but often interrupt work, cause accidental corruption of a file, damage the reputation of a company, or take up precious space and time as you try to remove them from a computing system. Just one virus infection can erase the contents of a drive, corrupt important files, or shut down a network.

The costs of removing viruses from a system are also increasing. A recent study by *Computer Economics* found that corporations spent $12.1 billion in 1999 to fight off viruses and other malware. Many corporations are now funding and installing antivirus solutions on a regular basis, accepting antivirus as a basic business need. At the same time, the expectations for funded antivirus solutions are higher—there is a demand for better protection, easier to use software, and more comprehensive security solutions.

A 1999 Computer Virus Prevalence Survey, conducted by ICSA.net, indicated that roughly 81 percent of all viruses were introduced by an e-mail attachment or a disk from home. Risky behaviors, such as blindly opening attachments from any source, not updating antivirus programs, and not verifying the correct operation of software, greatly increase the likelihood that a system will become infected with a virus.

Interpreting the threat

Several sources have estimated that there are more than 40,000 viruses in existence at the time of writing this book. At first, one may feel overwhelmed by such a daunting number. However, when one looks more closely at the statistical interpretation of this number, it becomes less daunting and more manageable.

The idea that there are 40,000 viruses in existence is an overwhelming thought, often marketed by the same individuals that develop and sell antivirus software. There is some controversy over how antivirus companies track and count viruses. For example, some companies count only families and major variants, while others count every single variant, no matter how insignificant, dramatically increasing the total number of viruses reported to be in existence.

Taking a closer look at what makes up a virus threat, we see that some viruses live only in the laboratory of an antivirus software engineer. Viruses that are in a controlled laboratory are often referred to as "In the Zoo" viruses. Viruses that are a threat to computer users are referred to as "In the Wild." The WildList organization at http://www.wildlist.org/faq.htm defines a virus In the Wild as one that "must be spreading as a result of normal day-to-day operations on and between the computers of unsuspecting users." For the purpose of this book, In the Wild (ItW) refers specifically to a virus that is listed in the WildList.

Over time, some viruses become extinct In the Wild, for all practical purposes, and are not considered a threat. For example, many older Macintosh viruses do not function correctly on System 7.0 or later. On PCs, many DOS file-infecting viruses are no longer as functional or successful in the Windows operating system. Still, older viruses continue to work on older operating systems and remain a threat for users of older systems. Antivirus efforts for users of older systems are often very different from those for users with newly updated systems.

Another important element in understanding the statistics of viruses is the concept of virus families. Viruses in a family are closely related by code, but vary in small ways. The once prevalent PC virus Stoned has so many similar variants within the family that some developers simply give them numbers, such as - Stoned-10, Stoned-11, and Stoned-12. On the Macintosh, the virus Merryxmas has a simple variant called Merry2xmas that differs only in the spelling of a comment tag and correction of an error contained within the original Merryxmas virus script. In many cases, simple variants of a family are easily detected and not as great a threat as new virus families found In the Wild.

Users have to know enough about how viruses are classified and categorized to understand the threats they face. Many of the 5 to 10 new viruses that are discovered each day are actually simple variants of a known virus In the Wild. For example, an individual may get a copy of a macro virus, edit it to insert his first name, and post it to an Internet source for distribution In the Wild. Such a similar variant within a virus family is often detected by an updated antivirus package that already detects the original virus of the family.

Much of the truly complex and malicious malware is not even In the Wild when it is reported by the media. Worms like BubbleBoy may get international press, but exist only In the Zoo or on underground Internet sites. However, users should take heed of such reports to avoid known security exploits and virus technology. In the past, several viruses, or their technology, have found their way into the Wild. Kak.Worm is an example of a worm recently discovered In the Wild that uses BubbleBoy technology.

Some viruses contain errors or delete themselves with a malicious payload, negatively affecting replication efforts. Other viruses infect only a handful of computers before being isolated In the Wild.

Given all these considerations, is there really a threat In the Wild today? Absolutely—data from the WildList and case studies such as the 1999 Melissa outbreak clearly prove this point. Traditionally, about 200 to 300 viruses have been considered to be In the Wild and an actual threat at any one time. Less than 50 of these are common, resulting in most of the reported infections worldwide.

New malware and security exploits are being created every day, even as you read this book. Becoming educated and taking action on the foundations of security and antivirus is essential for a safe computing experience.

Foreword

Computer viruses—a global problem that has been recognized only for a few years. Yet today almost all computer users have heard about them, and many are truly scared by them.

Viruses are no longer a distant future threat, they are already here and causing widespread damage. They have changed from random nuisance to normal part of everyday life. It's already business-as-usual for any medium-sized company to run into viruses if not daily at least weekly.

The big change with viruses started in the middle of 1990s, when macro viruses arrived. The Internet revolution only made the problem worse, with users being able to send an infected file across the world in seconds with just few clicks of the mouse.

However, viruses are a problem created by man and it's a problem that can be controlled by man. In the end, it's basically a war between virus writers and virus fighters. There are some bright minds on both sides, and it looks like this fight is going to last a while.

I work in a computer virus lab, unassembling computer code to discover and analyze computer viruses. It is interesting work—sometimes resembling playing chess. After a decade in this line of business, I haven't had a boring day yet. I really like that I can help people when they need it. During holidays, it's nice to receive post cards from people you've helped over the year to restore their computers, knowing that the other side—the virus writers—won't be getting any such cards.

The way to control the damage caused by viruses is to learn what viruses are, how they work, who writes them and why—and how you can protect your computer from an infection. This is what this book will teach you.

I leave you to dive into the strange and mysterious world of computer viruses. Get prepared for a fight.

In May 2000,
In the Lab,
In Finland,
Mikko H. Hypponen
Manager, Anti-Virus Research
F-Secure Corporation

1

History of Viruses

Computer viruses were explored by a variety of individuals in the computing industry during the 1960s and 1970s. Viruses were formally defined by Fred Cohen, in 1983, when he conducted a computer security experiment. A few years later, in 1986, the first formal PC computer virus, Brain, found its way into the Wild. Brain is a boot-sector virus that infects 360K floppy disks.

By the end of 1986, the Virdem and Burger file-infecting viruses were created as proof-of-concept viruses. The concepts of viruses and security exploits were now tangible, with example code available to interested parties.

It was in 1987 that the first real wave of virus attacks on computers In the Wild took place. Universities all around the world suffered outbreaks as students transferred files and disks from computer to computer. One of the best-known viruses today, Jerusalem, was discovered at the Hebrew University of Israel in 1987.

In 1988, virus infections became newsworthy in a big way. The Internet Worm, created by Robert T. Morris at Cornell University, was released In the Wild. John McAfee reported that it caused an estimated

$98,253,260 in damages. People familiar with the case, however, estimated damages closer to $1 million. An official Cornell University report claims that John McAfee, the individual who created the $98,253,260 estimate, "was probably serving [him]self" in an effort to drum up business (according to Rob Rosenberger at http://kumite.com/myths/myths/myth015.htm). Malware became newsworthy, prompting reports from *Byte*, *Business Week*, *Fortune*, *PC Computing*, *Time*, and *US News & World Report*. Corporate America and the government were now under attack, and everyone wanted to know about it.

An estimated 30 viruses were in existence by 1989. The foundation for a new industry, antivirus and security software, had been laid. Individuals such as Joe Wells, a leading antivirus consultant, got their start in the late 1980s and early 1990s. Programmers creating software to detect viruses, including heuristic programs to find new and previously undiscovered viruses In the Wild, had plenty of job security.

Programmers in the underground were just as busy creating new viruses. Individuals with strange names, such as Dark Avenger, began to be reported in the news. In the early 1990s, polymorphic, armored, and multipartite viruses joined the ranks of types of viruses found In the Wild. A coordinated effort emerged online, as underground authors began to trade viruses, codes, and ideas with one another through bulletin boards and Usenet newsgroups.

The Apple Macintosh operating system made a major update in 1990, going to System 7.0. This effectively eliminated most of the previous virus threats, since they were incompatible with the new operating system. PC users were still using the traditional operating system upon which original PC viruses were based.

To help coordinate antivirus efforts, the European Institute for Computer Antivirus Research (EICAR) was created in Hamburg in December 1990. This group exchanged antivirus ideas and later released the EICAR test file, used to validate the correct operation of installed antivirus software.

Virus authors fought back with sophisticated Virus Creation Center (VCC) tools that let just about any computer user make a computer virus. Programs such as the Mutation Engine (MtE), Virus Creation Laboratory (VCL), and Phalcon/Skism Mass-Produced Code Generator were all made available through the underground. Over 1000 viruses were in existence by the end of the year. By 1992 the first Windows virus, WinVir, was discovered In the Wild.

Microsoft released MS-DOS 6.0 in 1993. MS-DOS 6.2 included MSAV, an antivirus protection program that did little for the antivirus industry. That same year, Joe Wells posted his first official "WildList," listing all of the verified viruses In the Wild. Also, SatanBug, created by a minor, was discovered in Washington, D.C. Viruses like Monkey, which use encryption and also infect the master boot record of hard disks, began to change the rules of the game for virus removal and recovery of infected media. Merryxmas, a common Macintosh HyperCard virus In the Wild, also appeared in 1993, discovered by the author of this book.

The success of computers, networking, and the Internet in the 1990s hampered antivirus efforts. Once everyone was connected through a virtual community, and people could easily share files and disks with one another, viruses spread rampantly through the Wild. The timing of the release of macro viruses in 1995, starting with the Concept virus, was perfect, and the replication strategy was highly effective. Infecting Microsoft Word documents, macro viruses could be transferred to both Macintosh and PC operating platforms through infected Word files shared by disk or e-mail.

The antivirus software industry and corporate America fell behind in protecting against viruses In the Wild. Companies like Microsoft were embarrassed by the release of two commercial CDs containing the Concept virus. Protection policies, education, and antivirus software were barely in place, if at all, in many corporations worldwide.

By the end of 1996, macro viruses held the number one spot as the most prevalent type of virus In the Wild. With the sudden explosion of viruses In the Wild, the media again found viruses to be very newsworthy. The fear of viruses had been placed in the hearts and minds of millions of computer users worldwide. Just about everyone knew someone who had a virus experience or knew of a malicious program that wiped out everything on a computer.

The last few years of the millennium produced new exploits involving both Macintosh and PC operating systems. The Autostart worm, the first significant virus for the Macintosh system to be created in four years, was released in 1998. Internet users started to experience denial-of-service attacks from new technologies like Java and JavaScript. Worms, such as Melissa and Happy99.exe (SKA), spread rapidly through e-mail.

The millennium ended with a solid foundation of fear instilled into the average computer user. So much technology change in such a short period of time has left people wondering, "What can computers ultimately do?" Computers have become an invaluable resource for the average home and corporate user. The fear of losing a few hours, or the big report for the boss, is a valid fear as users become dependent upon computer technology.

Computer Virus Historical Timeline

1970   First notes on viruses

1986   Brain: First PC virus

1988   Internet Worm

1991   First polymorphic viruses

1992   Michelangelo hysteria

1992   WinVir: First Windows virus

1993   MS-DOS 6 and MSAV

1995   Concept: First Microsoft Word macro virus

1996   First Windows 95 virus

1996   Microsoft Excel macro viruses

1997   First Windows NT virus

1998   Microsoft Access macro viruses

1999   New era for malware

2

Malware

Malware is a generic term that covers a wide range of unwanted software: computer viruses, denial-of-service attacks, droppers, trojans, worms, and more. Putting parts of two words, MALicious and softWARE, together produces the word *malware*. The idea is that any software created on a computer for "bad" or malicious purpose is malware. Some malware, such as the Concept macro virus, only replicates, while viruses like Chernobyl (CIH family) may erase the contents of a hard drive.

Joke programs, such as Joke.Win.Stupid, are sometimes included in the definition of malware. Joke programs and hoaxes are often created in order to play a joke on someone else, without malicious intent. Actual spam, such as e-mail hoaxes like PenPal Greetings, is not software and does not meet the official definition of malware. However, some users may panic when they read an e-mail warning of a computing meltdown. When panic sets in, a user may shut off the computer incorrectly, potentially damaging files, the operating system, or even hardware components like the hard drive. Hoaxes may cost even more when Information Technology staff believes a hoax and spends countless worker-hours to prevent, contain, and protect against a threat that doesn't actually exist.

Easter eggs, hidden signatures sometimes added to software by programmers, are generally not considered malware. Sometimes an Easter egg is found by pressing certain keys or by a logic argument, such as the day of the month. True Easter eggs are designed to be fun (not malicious or frightening), sometimes revealing more about the author of the program.

Understanding the foundation of malware can help many users to avoid malware incidents and to differentiate real threats from simple jokes, hoaxes, or normal system issues. For example, a general protection fault (GPF) recognized by Dr. Watson software is something that an experienced computer user will recognize as a normal part of life in the Windows environment. Inexperienced users will often fear the worst, interpreting the GPF as a virus infection. Education on the basics of computing, software configuration, conflicts, and bugs goes a long way toward producing an enjoyable computing experience.

Bugs are also not included in the definition of malware. A bug is a programming error that results in partial or complete failure of an operation or program. The origin of the word *bug* is commonly associated with the team of individuals working with Professor Howard Aiken of Harvard, who found that a moth had short-circuited the wiring system on the Mark I computer. Programmers often "debug" software to identify and fix problem areas in the script prior to releasing new or updated software.

The well-known Year 2000 (Y2K) problem is neither a bug nor malware. Actually, it is the result of a programming shortcut. Instead of tracking all four digits of the year, such as 1979, programmers created programs that tracked only the last two digits, such as "79" for 1979. When working under heavy deadlines, some programmers had little time to worry about anything but their immediate financial gain and project deadlines. Unfortunately, many manufacturers continued to use "shortcut" code well into the 1990s, resulting in the need for costly upgrades of anything run by a computer or chip that was not Y2K compatible. Luckily the year 2000 New Year's Eve celebration was not dampened by Y2K; few problems were reported worldwide.

Computer Viruses

A computer virus is a program that is designed to replicate, spreading from computer to computer via host programs and sometimes carrying out a malicious action (payload). There are many types of viruses with various characteristics for avoiding detection, replicating, and carrying out a payload on a computer.

Naming conventions

Viruses go by a variety of names, some of which make more sense than others. While the CARO group, an elite set of antivirus researchers, attempted to set naming conventions in the early 1990s, there is no current international standard in place for the naming of new malware. For example, one antivirus program may report a virus as V-Sign while another reports that same virus as Cansu. Fortunately, most companies adopt similar names immediately after the initial discovery of a new virus. For example, the Concept virus is also known as WM.Concept.

Leading companies in the field, such as Symantec, publish their naming conventions online. Symantec names all viruses with a prefix that denotes the platform of replication, the family name, and a suffix for variants of a family, as applicable. For example, WM.Concept.C is a Word macro virus in the Concept family, variant C.

How Viruses Replicate

Viruses lie in wait on a computer, replicating to a local or networked drive when executed (run). At this very moment, there are thousands of viruses lying in wait on computers all around the world, waiting to be executed. Once the code is run, the virus may infect the system and spread to other files, disks (including network-accessible drives), boot sectors, and other computer media.

Code execution

Any time a new source medium enters a system, it puts the system at risk for a virus infection. When a user performs an action such as opening a new file, using a floppy disk, or running a new program downloaded from the Internet, a virus code may be executed, enabling a virus to infect and spread throughout the system.

Some viruses look for common files to infect, such as the foundational template document used with Microsoft (MS) Word, `normal.dot`. Others perform searches on a computer for file types, such as looking for `.exe` and `.com` extensions.

Parasitic attachment to host file

Viruses parasitically attach themselves to an existing host file on a computer. For example, if a game titled `tank.exe` has 10,000 bytes of code, it may have 12,000 bytes of code after a virus has infected the program.

When the infected program is run, the virus code is executed along with the `tank.exe` code. The virus is dependent upon the host program and is able to spread through a system only by attaching itself to existing files. Once a virus is run, it spreads to another file on the system and may also attempt to run in memory.

Viruses that run in memory

Terminate and stay resident (TSR) DOS viruses attempt to run in memory after being launched from the infected host file. Once the virus code is in memory, it works to infect a variety of files throughout the system until the computer is shut down. It may also work to conceal its presence from the user or from antivirus software installed on the computer.

Many TSR viruses attempt to infect startup files, so that the virus can be run in memory again when the computer is restarted at a later time.

Macro virus replication

When an infected Microsoft Word file is opened, macro virus code is executed. Macro viruses like Cap quickly work to conceal themselves by doing things such as disabling the *Macro* menu option under the *Tools* menu. At the same time, they work to infect `normal.dot` on the PC or `normal` on the Macintosh, Microsoft Word's default global template, which is opened every time Microsoft Word is launched.

Every Microsoft Word file that is opened after the initial infection will normally be infected with the macro virus. This is an extremely effective method for spreading a virus through a networked system, since Microsoft Word files are commonly exchanged between users. Macro viruses are able to control the environment upon the launching of Microsoft Word, infecting every document opened or created, sometimes going undetected for long periods of time.

Provided that the user doesn't experience any side effects of payloads from the virus infection, he or she will probably back up files to a disk. Once the user does remove the virus from the system, it is often reintroduced with a backup file at a later time. This is why it is so important for users to install on-access scanning software, which helps to protect against infection while the user works on the computer. A user who relies upon occasional manual scanning may reinfect his or her own system and continue to spread a macro virus for long periods of time.

Viruses focus on replication

Viruses focus more on replication than on destruction or stealing of sensitive data. The whole idea of the traditional virus is to infect as many files as possible, spreading to as many computers and networks worldwide as possible. With such a philosophy, destructive payloads are not often seen.

Far less than 10 percent of all viruses prevalent In the Wild carry a malicious payload. While some viruses may clog up a mail server or corrupt a file upon being removed from a system, they are not designed to damage a system. Viruses that are designed to be malicious, such as Chernobyl and Love Letter virus, are not as common but do get major headlines when they are found either In the Zoo or In the Wild.

Fortunately, most highly destructive viruses are not as prolific In the Wild as was the Chernobyl virus in 1999 and Love Letter in 2000.

It is important to note that the Chernobyl virus was a huge force in Asia, wiping out as many as 600,000 estimated computers on April 26, 1999 and Love Letter in 2000. In part, Asia suffered the wrath of the Chernobyl because of black market sales and a lack of proactive actions. A large majority of affected users had purchased illegally reproduced operating system CDs that had the Chernobyl virus on the disk. The United States reported few Chernobyl virus outbreaks as a result of not having the same black market environment and of aggressive media reports and proactive corporate and home user actions.

New security exploits

As technology changes, so do the exploits. Many new technologies, such as cookies and JavaScript, have users concerned about new types of computer malware. While cookies are not executable, JavaScript is a good example of how a new code is able to maliciously fool and disrupt a user's working environment on a computer. JavaScript is capable of running in an Internet browser to display false messages and warnings, open windows continuously until a memory problem occurs, or even shut down the browser.

Other new threats, such as BubbleBoy, exploit a bug to infect a system. A seemingly simple feature, such as Auto-Preview in the MS Outlook e-mail programs, when combined with improper security controls, puts a computer at risk. With Auto-Preview, when an e-mail is selected, the program automatically runs a code to display the message in a preview pane. New malware like BubbleBoy uses such an action to infect a system with a virus or drop an infection script into the start-up folder on the hard drive.

Why Viruses Are Created

Viruses were originally explored by researchers to see if such exploits and software behavior were possible on a computer system. In today's world, viruses are created for a wide variety of reasons, ranging from the challenge of it all to cyberwarfare.

Profile of a virus author

Virus authors range from children to adults. Most of them are male, and they fall into three main age categories: adolescent, young adult (college), and adult (generally less than 40 years of age). The motivations of the three age groups vary. The average programmer of viruses does not have advanced skills. More advanced programmers sometimes belong to groups such as 29A.

Common motivations

The act of creating a virus is considered irresponsible, but the morality of most virus authors involves a certain amount of justification of their wrongdoing. Some professional virus programmers only work to expose security holes or to create malware that will be noted by the press or listed in Joe Wells' WildList.

Common motivations for creating malware include fame and pride, challenge, and vandalism. A list of possible motivations are listed below:

- *Fame and pride.* Press coverage, how prolific a virus is In the Wild, what gets infected with a virus, being the first to exploit a new security hole or method of infection, and special payloads that a virus may deliver bring a certain amount of fame and pride to some virus authors.

- *Challenge.* Many virus-creation enthusiasts desire and enjoy the technical challenge.

- *Revenge/vandalism.* Some viruses are specifically designed to strike back at a specific company or individual. Disgruntled employees have been known to create malware and plant it in the workplace to disrupt the working environment when they have a grievance or have been fired from a position with a company. Other virus creators are simply vandals, with no purpose other than to destroy and damage computing systems.

- *Power.* Authors may feel a sense of power when they create programs that have the capability to overwrite data or capture sensitive information.

- *Exposing security holes.* Some programmers use malware as a way of proving a point about a security hole in a software package.

- *Financial gain.* Stock prices of antivirus software corporations sometimes fluctuate based upon virus outbreaks and events.

- *Espionage/raiders.* Obtaining embargoed, confidential information about company initiatives, governments, the military, and other targets of attack motivates some programmers.

- *Cyberwar / terrorism.*   Some governments are using malware as an offensive tool. Technology is at the center of many new military initiatives and tools of war, which are subject to unauthorized access and attack. Terrorists may also use malware to attack critical support features of society that utilize computer technology, such as electricity, transportation, and the stock market.

- *Fun and foolishness.*   Many simple variants of a common virus are created by adolescents who are simply playing around. Adding the name of a friend to the code, editing code to be "cool," or striving for attention from fellow computing enthusiasts are common examples of children simply having a bit of irresponsible foolish fun.

- *Emotional needs.*   Some antivirus authors have a variety of unmet emotional needs that drive them to create viruses for a sense of self-identification, value, and life in the world as they know it. Becoming part of the elusive underground community is an important element of life for authors motivated by unmet emotional needs.

- *Education.*   Some instructors teach students how to program viruses as an exercise in learning programming. Others work with virus codes to help educate others about what viruses are and how they work, incidentally encouraging virus creation.

- *Accidental / bug.*   Variants of existing viruses In the Wild are sometimes created by accidental editing. Programmers may also accidentally create a virus-like script when developing and debugging software.

Antivirus Laws and Justice

When an entire corporation is shut down because of a virus, or files are deleted from a home computer, people begin the search for justice! Unfortunately, there is little or no justice done most of the time. Because most viruses don't do much except annoy users or carry out a harmless payload, it isn't always that important to track down a virus author to bring him or her to justice. The expense and difficulty of investigating and tracking down such an author just isn't worth it most of the time.

Is it justice?

Once malware authors are found, are they convicted, and do the sentences provide justice? You decide, after reviewing the examples in Table 2.1.

Grounds for prosecution vary from region to region worldwide but may include

- Unauthorized access or modification made to a system
- Fraud
- Injurious, including terrorism
- Loss of data
- Endangering the safety of others
- Denial of service
- Obscene and indecent media

Viral terrorism—A new war to fight

Viral terrorism—fighting wars and promoting political agendas with malware—is an idea that has been around for a long time. As computers are integrated into military, corporate, and other establishments, people become more dependent upon them for basic services as well as for information and communication. Attacking such sources is the specialty of online cyberterrorists.

A good example of how formalized cyber attacks have become comes from Asia, where Lieutenant

TABLE 2.1
Malware Authors and Sentencing

Author	Justice?
Robert T. Morris 1988, released Internet worm Estimated damage $1,000,000 to $98,253,260	3 years probation 400 hours community service $10,050 fine plus cost of supervision
Christopher Pile **(AKA Black Baron)** 1995, released SMEG viruses Violated Computer Misuse Act of the United Kingdom Estimated damage exceeding 500,000 pounds	18 months in prison
Chen Ing-hau 1999, released Chernobyl virus 600,000 to 2,500,000 computers struck by the virus, which attempts to erase the contents of hard drives and the BIOS.	Confessed but suffers no conse- quences. "He's not a criminal here as long as no one registers a complaint," a Taipei police spokeswoman said. International users affected by the Chernobyl virus have no prosecuting rights.
Kevin Mitnick Unauthorized access to computers and data Estimated damage $296,000,000.	Sentenced on August 9, 1999, to 46 months in prison, fined $4125, not allowed to touch computers and other high tech- nology devices for 3 years, and not allowed to discuss the case for 7 years. Released in January 2000 after having served almost four and a half years in prison prior to the sentencing.
David Smith 1999, released Melissa worm Prolific In the Wild, shutting down multiple e-mail servers of major corporations Estimated damage $80,000,000	Pleaded guilty in 1999. Faces 40 years in jail and fines up to $480,000. Sentencing to occur in the year 2000.
Onel de Guzman (suspect) 2000, released Love Letter worm Estimated damage $7,000,000,000 dollars	Prosecution pending for suspect who reportedly admits to writing the virus, but claims that he accidently introduced it to the Internet.

General Lin Chin-ching, head of the defense ministry's information and communications bureau of Taiwan, has categorized roughly 1000 different computer viruses. Taiwan reportedly has viruses ready to release in retaliation for any electronic attacks that may come from China. While such reports may be just propaganda, they clearly identify the threat of virus propaganda, and information warfare, as real and potentially useful in military efforts.

Characteristics of viruses

Each family of viruses has its own characteristics and methods of reproduction. Viruses have been categorized in a variety of ways based upon these characteristics. Most viruses have multiple characteristics that force them to be classified into several categories. For example, the One_Half virus is file-infecting and a master boot record infector (multipartite). Table 2.2 outlines major characteristics used in classification of viruses.

Stealth techniques—an inside look

Most malware is designed to remain hidden from the user after infection. Antivirus developers design antivirus software to look for exact identifications of viruses, changes in a system, and heuristics. Viruses are more likely to be successful in replication efforts when they infect a system without updated antivirus software.

One stealth technique is to infect a file only once. Many viruses, such as Thus.E, contain code that checks for a previous infection. If a previous infection is found, the virus does not attempt a second infection. This way, the virus author avoids duplicate infections and increased risk of detection of a virus on the infected system.

TABLE 2.2
Virus Characteristics

Virus Characteristics	Description
Armored Example: Whale	These viruses utilize advanced stealth techniques, such as encryption and movement of virus code, to avoid detection and disassembly analysis.
Boot-sector infector (BSI) Example: Form	These viruses infect the boot sector of a disk. Master boot record–infecting viruses may infect the boot sector of a floppy disk. Formatting an infected disk effectively removes a boot-sector virus. Master boot record viruses are not removed with the formatting of a disk. See the master boot record classification for more information.
Cavity virus Example: Lehigh	This type of virus attempts to infect a file without increasing the length of the file, overwriting selected portions of code in the host file while attempting to preserve functionality.
Companion virus Example: Aids II	This type of virus creates a companion file to run a virus program and the original program. Some companion viruses exploit the feature of DOS that leads it to always run files with `.com` extensions before those with `.exe`. Because it has the same exact name, but a `.com` extension, the companion virus program is always run first once it has infected a system. Other companion viruses rename a targeted program and create a virus program with the original target program name.
Encrypting Example: Monkey	Encryption is sometimes used by a virus to encrypt data or self-encrypt, as seen with polymor-

(*Continued*)

TABLE 2.2
Virus Characteristics (Continued)

Virus Characteristics	Description
	phic viruses. The Monkey virus infects the master boot record of a hard disk and encrypts the partition data to the drive. Files may be viewed only when Monkey is booted into memory, decrypting the partition data encrypted on the hard drive. Removing the Monkey virus also removes the ability to decipher the encrypted partition data on the drive, effectively erasing the contents of the drive. Special tools and techniques must be utilized to remove viruses like Monkey.
File Example: Jerusalem	This type of virus infects a file, such as an executable (.exe) program or Microsoft Word document (.doc). When the infected file is opened or the infected program is run, the virus is executed along with the instructions for the file. Microsoft Word document infections are more commonly referred to as macro viruses.
	Certain file types, such as image files (JPG, GIF) and movie files (MPEG), are not executables and do not pose a threat. However, some viruses masquerade as a "safe" file, such as JPG, in efforts to infect a system.
Fast/slow infectors (sparse) Example: Dark Avenger	Some viruses control the rate of infection in an attempt to avoid immediate removal from a system. Some are fast, such as Dark Avenger. Others are deliberately slow, infecting only a fraction of the time that they are executed. For example, a slow-infecting virus may infect only once out of 15 executions when run.

TABLE 2.2
Virus Characteristics (Continued)

Virus Characteristics	Description
HyperCard (Macintosh only) Example: Merryxmas	HyperCard is an open scripting environment in which users may use the HyperTalk language to program custom scripts, functions, and programs for the Macintosh computer. Much like the Visual Basic macros that affect Microsoft Word and other products, HyperCard viruses work only within a given program.
Macro Example: Concept	Macro viruses can execute only in programs that support macros. Microsoft Word and Excel are the most common programs infected with macro viruses, created in Visual Basic for Applications or WordBasic. Since the release of the first Microsoft Word macro virus, Concept, in 1995, macro viruses have grown at an incredible rate In the Wild. They are now the most prevalent type of virus found In the Wild.
Master boot record (MBR) Example: AntiCMOS	All hard disks contain a master boot record that is referenced by the computer when it starts up. MBR viruses infect the hard drive MBR with virus code when an infected disk is used to boot a computer.
	The most common way in which this happens is for a user to accidentally leave an infected disk in the computer during shutdown. When the computer next starts up, it attempts to boot from the floppy disk, infecting the hard drive with the MBR virus. Following infection, the MBR virus is run, along with the normal MBR code, when the computer is started up from the now

(Continued)

TABLE 2.2
Virus Characteristics (Continued)

Virus Characteristics	Description
	infected hard drive. MBR viruses then attempt to infect the boot sector of floppies and other disks as they are used.
	MBR viruses are not removed from a disk during the format process. Since the MBR resides in a different location on a disk, an MBR virus must be removed with a tool like FDISK or by booting the computer from a clean boot disk prior to using antivirus software to remove the virus.
Multipartite Example: Pieck	Multipartite viruses attempt to spread at a faster rate by infecting in more than one way. The most common method of multipartite viruses is to infect both a program and the master boot record. This type of virus is often very successful In the Wild but is rare In the Wild today. See the descriptions of file and master boot record viruses for more information.
Polymorphic Example: Hare	As the name implies, (*poly*, meaning "many," and *morphic*, meaning "shape"), polymorphic viruses contain complex instructions that enable them to mutate into new and different viruses within the same family. Detection of well-programmed polymorphic viruses can be very difficult. New heuristic methods have helped to detect and remove new and previously undiscovered polymorphic viruses In the Wild. Unfortunately, heuristics often have "false-positive" results, incorrect detection, when looking for "viruslike" code.

TABLE 2.2
Virus Characteristics (Continued)

Virus Characteristics	Description
Stealth Example: One_Half	These viruses attempt to conceal their presence on an infected system, so the virus can replicate and remain undetected for long periods of time. Stealth viruses may attempt to intercept system calls to report back information for an uninfected document, avoiding detection. CAP is a common macro virus that attempts to quietly hide macro menu options from the user to avoid detection. There are several well-known, but often rare, advanced stealth techniques, including armoring, cavity, and tunneling.
Terminate and stay resident (TSR) Example: Jerusalem	These DOS viruses run in memory upon being executed, even after the original host program is terminated. Following an infection, many TSR viruses are constructed to run in memory upon startup. This enables the TSR virus to run in memory each time the computer is run.
Tunneling	These viruses call original interrupt handlers in DOS and BIOS directly, bypassing monitoring programs that may be running to detect virus activity. Interestingly enough, some antivirus programs use the tunneling technique to bypass viruses that may be running in memory.

To avoid future infections, some antivirus programs leave an "inoculation script" in place when they remove a virus. If the virus attempts to reinfect the system at a later date, the inoculation script fools the virus so that it does not execute the infection attempt. One problem with leaving an inoculation script is that it is often detected as a virus by different antivirus programs. This may result in a false-positive (false alarm) report, confusing some users.

Another stealth technique is to write to a disk only when disk activity is detected on a system. This way, the user is less likely to notice extra drive activity on the infected computer.

Macro viruses—an inside look

Macro viruses are one of the most common types of viruses In the Wild today. They are easily transferred via e-mail and disk, contained within Word, Excel, and other macro-supporting programs. The first macro virus, Concept, was found In the Wild in 1995. Since that time, the number of macro viruses has exploded exponentially.

Macro viruses exploit the programming code of Visual Basic for Applications (VBA) and WordBasic, a programming language supported by programs like Microsoft Word. An example of VBA macro code that is used to change the font style, size, and color of selected text is shown below:

```
Sub Toggle ()
'
'Toggle Macro
'Macro recorded 03/12/00 by Ken Dunham
'
Selection.Font.Bold = wdToggle
Selection.Font.Size = 48
Selection.Font.Name = "Arial"
Selection.Font.ColorIndex = wdRed
End Sub
```

Sub and End Sub start and end the macro, respectively. The name of the macro, Toggle in this case, is on the third line of the subroutine script. The rest of the code changes the selected text to a size 48, Arial font, and a red color.

When a macro virus is edited by a novice, a simple change, such as changing 48 to 72, constitutes a new virus within a virus family. The trick to creating new

macro viruses is figuring out how to get them to replicate. This is often achieved by infecting `normal.dot`,
the startup file normally used with Microsoft Word
when the program is run. When Word is executed,
`normal.dot` is normally opened, with macros that
then run in memory while the user works.

Famous Malware

Even though there are an estimated 30,000 to 50,000
forms of malware in existence, a few stand out among
the crowd:

- AutoStart Worm
- Back Orifice
- Brain
- Chernobyl (CIH family)
- Class
- Concept
- Hare
- Jerusalem
- Love Letter
- Melissa
- Merryxmas
- Michelangelo
- Monkey
- Stoned
- Tequila
- Wazzu
- WDEF

Malware prevalency chart

Table 2.3 lists the malware most prevalent In the Wild
in the first quarter of 2000, based upon an analysis of
data posted by leading antivirus organizations. Only

TABLE 2.3
Malware Prevalent In the Wild, First
Quarter of 2000

Malware	Primary type
APS.21657	Trojan
Class	Macro
Ethan	Macro
Freelink	File/VBS script
Happy99.exe (SKA)	Worm
Kak.worm	Worm
Laroux	Macro
Marker	Macro
Melissa	Worm
Pretty Park	Worm/Trojan
Sub7Gold.21	Trojan
Tristate	Macro
VMPCK	Macro

the primary type for each piece of malware is listed when malware has more than one type of classification. For detailed definitions of malware other than viruses, see "Other Malware" later in this chapter.

Analysis of this prevalency chart identifies macro viruses as one of the most common primary types of viruses In the Wild in the first quarter of 2000.

Virus payloads (warheads)

Viruses employ a wide range of payloads, actions that take place during or after infection. Some payloads are malicious, while others may be humorous. Some viruses, such as Chernobyl, may infect a system and lie in wait for a given date or computing event before carrying out a destructive payload, such as attempting to delete all the files on the hard drive of the infected computer.

Ethan, a common macro virus, infects Microsoft Word documents and then changes the properties of infected files to present "Ethan Frome" as the suggested *save* name. Even after the Ethan virus is removed from a computer, the visual payload may still reside inside infected documents. A simple fix is to select *Properties* from the *File* menu and delete the "Ethan Frome" text, as shown in Fig. 2.1.

Whenever a user encounters an unusual message, new dialog box, or suspicious activity, it is important to log all the details of the event to aid in troubleshooting if it should be required.

Macintosh Viruses

Macintosh users often have difficulty finding an antivirus product, let alone information about Macintosh system viruses online. Antivirus developers have a tough time justifying the expense of developing and supporting an antivirus tool for Macintosh when the prospects of such a market are so small in comparison to the PC market.

For another thing, there are only a handful of Macintosh system viruses in existence, most of which are not a threat anymore (some qualifications are given below). Table 2.4 describes all Macintosh system malware families documented as of May 2000. Most are now obsolete, no longer a threat to the average Macintosh user.

While Macintosh system viruses are few in number, macro viruses are abundant In the Wild. Macintosh users who utilize Microsoft products, such as Word, are susceptible to macro viruses that infect both Macintosh and PC Microsoft applications. If HyperCard or HyperCard Player is used on a system, a HyperCard-specific antivirus may also be needed for best protection.

Macintosh users who make use of software and hardware emulation for PCs are exposed to unique virus risks. When a software emulation tool such as SoftWindows is used, a file is created on the Macintosh drive to emulate a PC hard disk. If the Macintosh user runs the emulation software and later

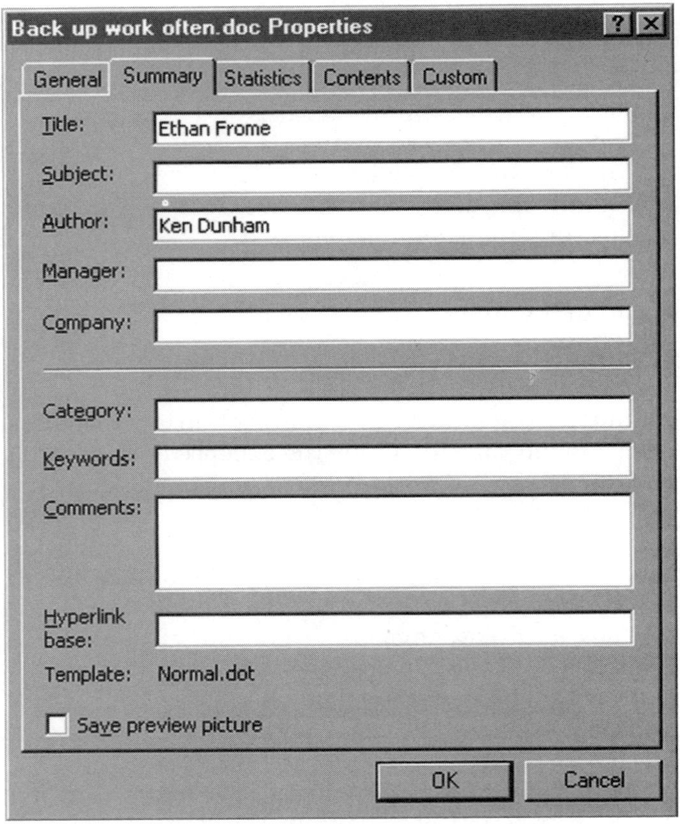

Figure 2.1 Update Word document properties to remove Ethan payload.

introduces new media to the computer, such as opening an attachment from e-mail accessed in the emulated PC environment, an infection may take place. Because the operation of an emulated environment is different from the real thing, some infections may fail. More importantly, PC system–specific viruses often fail when run in a Macintosh operating system.

PC boot-sector viruses will attempt to infect the hard disk only when run under a PC-emulated envi-

TABLE 2.4
Documented Macintosh System Malware

Macintosh system malware family	Description
Antibody	HyperCard virus (common). This virus may accidentally interrupt legitimate scripts that are being executed.
ANTI (ANTI A, ANTI B)	System virus (once common). ANTI often results in corruption of infected applications. Interestingly enough, ANTI A contains scripts to neutralize ANTI B, even though ANTI B was not discovered until 18 months later.
AppleScript Trojans	Trojan (uncommon). AppleScript is a powerful tool on the Macintosh. At least one example of a Trojan created in AppleScript was discovered in 1997; it was designed to compromise security on the infected Macintosh system.
Autostart 9805	Worm (common). Discovered in May of 1998, this worm quickly infected Macintosh computers all around the world. Following infection, computers may have data randomly overwritten by the worm.
	This worm is one of the primary Macintosh system–related threats existing today. Primary overt symptoms include "DB" flashing in the menu bar when a disk is mounted and extensive disk activity every 30 min.
Blink	HyperCard virus (once common). Common during its introduction, this virus is now considered rare. After infection, it makes active HyperCard windows "blink."
CDEF	System virus (once common). This virus is able to spread only under System 6.X and older versions. It may result in crashes after infec-

(*Continued*)

TABLE 2.4
Documented Macintosh System Malware (Continued)

Macintosh system malware family	Description
	tion. To remove this virus from the hard disk, simply rebuild the desktop with command-option during startup.
ChinaTalk	Trojan (once common). Mas xquerading as an INIT/Extension, this Trojan attempts to erase all drives upon startup following installation.
CODE 1	System virus (once common). This virus infects applications and the system file of Macintosh Systems 6.X and 7.X. It may rename the hard drive to "Trent Saburo" and result in some crashes or errors.
CODE 252	System virus (uncommon). This virus may display a threatening message but does nothing to the drive.
CODE 32767	System virus (uncommon). This destructive application-infecting virus may attempt to delete files on infected systems. The virus spreads by modifying the jump table entry CODE 0 of an infected program to point to CODE 32767.
CODE 9811	System virus (uncommon). This virus may display a red pi symbol and black wormlike lines on the screen following infection.
	Discovered in 1998, this virus is relatively new to the Macintosh operating system. It may corrupt infected applications.
Cpro	Trojan (once common). This destructive Trojan, which originally came in the form CPRO141.SEA, attempts to reformat drives when run. Fortunately, it is only successful at reformatting floppy disks.

TABLE 2.4
Documented Macintosh System Malware (Continued)

Macintosh system malware family	Description
Dukakis	HyperCard virus (uncommon). This virus displays the message *Dukakis for president in '88* and then deletes itself. It is now considered obsolete.
Esperanto	System virus (uncommon). This controversial virus has been reported by a few sources to have the capability to infect both Macintosh and PC systems. When executed under a PC emulation environment, such as SoftWindows, it reportedly has the capability to infect the Macintosh system with a virus. The author of this book has not been able to substantiate the claims made or to obtain a copy of the virus for testing purposes. It is not considered a real threat to the Macintosh system at the time of writing this book.
Flag (WDEF C)	System virus (uncommon). This virus infects the Macintosh system file (WDEF resource), working to infect all run programs following infection. This virus is different from standard WDEF virus infections because it infects the system file directly rather than relying upon a disk mount.
FontFinder	Trojan (uncommon). Running an application called FontFinder runs a Trojan that effectively scrambles data on the hard drive.
Frankie (Aladdin)	System virus (uncommon). Frankie infects only Macintosh emulators used on Atari computers. Frankie displays a bomb message with the text *Frankie says: No more piracy*! at the top of the Atari screen and then crashes the system.

(Continued)

TABLE 2.4
Documented Macintosh System Malware (Continued)

Macintosh system malware family	Description
HC 9507 (Pickle)	HyperCard virus (once common). This virus may result in crashes and display errors. Pickle may display the text *Pickle*.
HC 9603	HyperCard virus (uncommon). This virus may result in unpredictable script handling and execution.
Independance Day (Sic)	HyperCard virus (once common). Although it attempts to randomly delete lines of script from the Home stack, this virus is more of an embarrassment to the author who programmed this virus so badly—not to mention misspelling the word *independence*.
INIT 17	System virus (uncommon). This virus displays the message *From the depths of Cyberspace* and may crash the system.
INIT 29 (INIT 29 A, INIT 29 B)	System virus (once common). This may result in crashes or printing errors.
INIT 1984 (INIT M)	System virus (once common). Discovered In the Wild in 1993, this virus randomly changes file and folder names on any infected Macintosh computer booted on Friday the 13th with a system date of 1991 or later. Users of Macintosh 128K, 512K, and XL systems may have a crash upon startup following infection. If you have Disinfectant installed and an infected INIT, Disinfectant will beep ten times during startup and display an alert.
INIT 9403 (SysX)	System virus (uncommon). Rumors are that this virus was generated from an altered version of pirated software. This virus has been

TABLE 2.4
Documented Macintosh System Malware (Continued)

Macintosh system malware family	Description
	found only on Macintosh computers using the Italian version of Mac OS 6.X and 7.X.
MacMag (Aldus, Drew, Brandow, Peace)	System virus (uncommon). This virus originated in the Montreal offices of *MacMag* magazine. A HyperCard stack (dropper) called "New Apple Products" was used to infect the system file when it was run. No direct damage is associated with this virus.
MBDF (MBDF A, MBDF B)	System virus (once common). MBDF was originally spread in several game applications offered on the Internet, including 10 Tile Puzzle, Obnoxious Tetris, and Tetricycle/Tetris-rotating. System performance is negatively affected following infection.
MDEF (Garfield, Top Cat, MDEF A, MDEF B, MDEFC, MDEF D)	System virus (once common). This virus may damage files, with some variants causing processing errors. MDEF D beeps every time an infected file is run and can damage an application beyond repair.
Merryxmas (merry2xmas, crudshot, lopez, multiple other names in this family)	HyperCard virus (common). This is a very common HyperCard virus family. These viruses infect the Home stack and then infect all HyperCard stacks opened after infection. The virus immediately reinfects the Home stack or opened stacks if the virus script is removed from either location. One variant in particular, crudshot, is malicious by design. This virus was discovered by the author of this book.
Movie Booster	Trojan (uncommon). The author of this book has not been able to verify reports of this Trojan but has

(Continued)

TABLE 2.4
Documented Macintosh System Malware (Continued)

Macintosh system malware family	Description
	included it here to address messages posted to a 1998 newsgroup. A QuickTime movie file called Movie Booster, according to 1998 newsgroup messages, contained a Trojan. This Trojan reportedly creates several new files within various *System* folders on a Macintosh system and may adversely affect normal booting of a Macintosh system.
Mosaic	Trojan (uncommon). Mosaic promotes itself as a legitimate drawing program. When the program is run, it destroys the directories of any SCSI-connected volume, effectively wiping out the hard volume. It then renames the destroyed volume "Gotcha."
nVir (nVIR A, nVIR B, nVIR-F, nCAM, Hpat, MEV#, nFLUE, Jude, AIDS, prod, modm, zero, clap) No Vowels Prank (NVP)	System virus (once common). This virus may say *don't panic*, beep upon startup or when an infected application is run, or delete files within the *System* folder.
	Trojan (uncommon). This virus may limit the keyboard so that the user cannot type vowels.
Postscript Hack	Trojan (uncommon). This virus may toggle the PostScript printer password.
Scores (Eric, Vult, NASA, San Jose Flu)	System virus (once common). This virus is rumored to have been created by a disgruntled programmer, with the aim of harming two applications under development at his former company. It changes icons and may cause problems with printing or correct operation of programs. It is not believed to be a threat at this time.

TABLE 2.4
Documented Macintosh System Malware (Continued)

Macintosh system malware family	Description
SevenDust (A-G, Graphics Accelerator, MDEF 9806 A-B, MDEF 666)	System virus (uncommon). This virus was originally discovered on Info-Mac downloads in 1998. Several variants of this polymorphic family are malicious, attempting to destroy files on the hard drive. MDEF 9806-B deletes non-application files every 6 months.
Steroid	Trojan (uncommon). This virus initializes the boot sectors of all volumes, up to 32,768 total volumes.
T4 (T4-A, T4-B, T4-C, T4-Beta)	System virus (uncommon). This virus may damage programs and cause a system to become unbootable. Versions 2.0 and 2.1 of the GoMoku game contain the T4 virus.
Tetracycle	Dropper (uncommon). Tetracycle masquerades as a game to drop the MBDF virus onto a Macintosh system.
Three Tunes (two tunes)	HyperCard virus (uncommon). This virus may display the message *Hey, what are you doing*? and *Don't panic*! as well as playing musical tunes. This virus is now considered obsolete.
Virus Info	Trojan (uncommon In the Wild). This virus scrambles the directory structures on the drive from which it is run, often the hard drive.
WDEF (WDEF A, WDEF B)	System virus (once common). WDEF works only on System 6.X. All other systems, 7.X and up, are immune to this virus. This was one of the first Macintosh viruses to be widespread, infecting thousands of Macintosh disks in the late 1980s. Infections sometimes result in corruption of data on a floppy disk. Hold down command-option while

(Continued)

TABLE 2.4
Documented Macintosh System Malware (Continued)

Macintosh system malware family	Description
	inserting the disk to rebuild the desktop and remove this virus from the disk. Make sure you do the same thing while booting from the hard drive to remove the virus from the hard disk too.
Wormcode	HyperCard virus (recently discovered). Posted to comp.sys.mac.hypercard Usenet group on 2/19/00 in a stack called Font Preview, this virus exploits the open-stack handler to infect HyperCard stacks. Like Merryxmas, this virus has no malicious payload and is easily prevented with a simple inoculation script at the end of the Home stack script, **end openstack —home script 2** (exactly as it appears in bold, no leading hyphens).
ZUC (ZUC A, ZUC B, ZUC C)	System virus (uncommon). This virus may produce strange cursor behavior at various times and slow program launch.

ronment. Simply inserting a PC-formatted disk into a Macintosh computer, with no emulator running, poses no threat of PC boot-sector virus infection.

While some infections may fail, viruses may still be present on a system. Because Macintosh system viruses are different from PC system viruses, PC viruses may go undetected on a Macintosh system, and vice versa. This may result in a user's unintentionally passing on an infected disk or file to a native environment, resulting in an infection on a different machine. For example, a Macintosh user at home may have an infected PC-formatted disk that does not infect the Macintosh system but does infect a PC system at work.

Because of the unique risks, all Macintosh users with emulated environments should be careful to have antivirus solutions for both the Macintosh and PC environments in place on their computers.

Other Malware

The distinctions among various forms of viruses and other malware are more technical distinctions than anything else. The average user is simply concerned about malware entering a system, not about the technical details of how the way one type of malware infects or spreads across a network differs from the way another type does so.

Malware is defined in this book to help users understand terms that are sometimes used in news media and security reports. The primary focus of all users should be the protection of a system against malware, rather than understanding all the technical distinctions of malware itself.

Trojan horse programs

Trojan horse programs are executables that masquerade as legitimate programs, often compromising security or executing a malicious payload on the affected computer. For example, a user opens on a Trojan masquerading as a game, titled `tank.exe`, which immediately deletes files on the hard drive.

Many Trojans avoid executing payloads that immediately erase files on a drive. Such an immediate and overt action results in immediate discovery and may remove the Trojan itself. The result is a slow transfer of the Trojan In the Wild, making such Trojans rare. Trojans with delayed malicious or hidden payloads, such as stealing passwords, are harder to detect and are increasingly prevalent In the Wild today. Because new Trojans are often more difficult for traditional antivirus programs to detect, they are likely to enjoy a consistent rise in prevalency In the Wild.

Trojans are often received as e-mail attachments or gifts from a friend on a disk. Other times, a program called a dropper "drops" the Trojan onto a computer (this is rare). Droppers are sometimes designed to get past antivirus solutions, enabling malware to be installed on a computer. If a dropper places malware into memory only, it is sometimes called an injector.

Removal of a Trojan is easy: Simply delete the file in question. Unfortunately, after having been run on a system, some Trojans may remain in memory or may have corrupted files or configured the computer to run code upon startup. For example, some Trojans are designed to steal passwords, watching events on the computer while a user works and then sending information to an e-mail or other location on the Internet—all without the user's knowledge. In such situations, a more detailed scan with an updated antivirus program or an alternative antivirus or anti-Trojan program or obtaining specific removal instructions for the Trojan may be necessary in order to remove all portions of the malware on the infected computer. If the Trojan corrupts or deletes files, restoring from a backup file may be necessary.

Worms

A worm is much like a virus, but it does not require a host program. A typical file virus will attach itself to the existing code of a file or program. Worms may make complete copies of themselves and spread through a network quickly, without parasitically attaching themselves to any existing files or programs.

There are two types of worms, host computer worms and network worms. Host computer worms, sometimes called "rabbits," use a network connection to spread through a network, running on only one computer at one time. The Internet Worm created by Robert Morris in 1988 is a host computer worm.

Network worms run on more than one computer on an infected network at a time. Each infection on the network is sometimes referred to as a "segment," with the segments making up the "body" of a network worm. Each segment may work independently, or the segments may work together, with a segment coordinating "body actions" across a network. Network worms that have a segment coordinating the work of other segments are sometimes called "octopuses."

Because of the way worms replicate, they often spread quickly through networked environments and e-mail. E-mail worms are a rather new and quickly increasing type of malware In the Wild, regularly infecting large numbers of users. Happy99.exe, Melissa, and Pretty Park are just a few of the more recent examples that have been plaguing Internet e-mail users for several months.

Internet Relay Chat (IRC) programs have been known to have worms specifically attack them. mIRC, a component of IRC that enables users to send files to one another, has been exploited by worms several times. Simsalapim is a well-known example of one such exploit.

Bombs and Service Attacks

ANSI bomb.   An ANSI bomb exploits ANSI technology to issue a command like `format c:`. While few computers have ANSI consoles today, many computers do have an `ANSI.SYS` file. ANSI bombs are rare, partly due to the fact that most programs do not make use of the `ANSI.SYS` file today.

Logic bomb.   Logic bombs are often attached to a working program but do not replicate. Much like a delayed payload from a virus, a logic bomb lies in wait on a computer until a specific condition is met. For example, if it is a certain day of a given month, the logic bomb may attempt to delete the contents of a hard drive.

Bacterium.   A program that replicates exponentially in an effort to exhaust processor capabilities, memory, or disk space is called a bacterium. If the program is successful, the computer will probably crash and may suffer a variety of integrity issues surrounding the crash event, as well as there being little memory and/or available hard drive space left. This term is rarely used today.

Other security threats

ICQ. ICQ is a program that enables Internet users to chat; send messages, files, and Internet links to one another; and even play games remotely. Some users of ICQ engage in conversations with malicious individuals who send them Internet addresses with malware attacks, such as a service attack via JavaScript. Others may accept files from an ICQ user, sometimes resulting in infection of their computer by a virus or Trojan. ICQ has a variety of security holes that may be exploited by malware authors and hackers.

Java. Java is a language developed by Sun Systems, Inc., to produce interactive cross-platform applications within files called *applets*. Java applets may contain malicious code that can cause service errors and other malware-type attacks. StrangeBrew was the first Java-infecting virus to be developed In the Zoo, but it is not able to infect Java applets. Because Java applets operate within a protected "sandbox" on a computer and Java has been updated several times since StrangeBrew was first introduced, no real Java-based threat currently exists In the Wild at the time of writing this book. Still, most Internet browsers have a security option to block or disable the running of any Java applet encountered on a Web page or computer.

JavaScript. JavaScript is a language developed by Netscape, Inc., to increase interactivity and control on Internet Web pages. JavaScript is totally different from Java, working more like a plug-in to an Internet browser. While JavaScript is able to produce powerful scripts, it does not support the development of complete programs like those that can be created in Java.

JavaScript is most often used to create simple rollover effects and dynamic menus on Internet Web pages. In the last few months, you may have noticed a Web page in which the text changed color or showed a glowing background as you moved the mouse over the top of it. If so, it was probably JavaScript that made the color or image change.

JavaScript controls objects, such as windows, graphics, and forms. JavaScript can be used to fool a user into thinking that he or she has a virus or that the hard drive is being reformatted. Simple tricks include presenting a message like *Warning! Hard Drive Being Formatted!* in the status bar or as an alert window. Another, and more serious, issue is when JavaScript is used to open up a huge number of windows, eventually making the computer run low on memory and bombing the machine. Such a situation can damage the hard drive and software on the machine. While there are no true JavaScript viruses In the Wild at this time, JavaScript certainly can perform denial-of-service attacks and create great fear in users online.

ActiveX.   ActiveX controls are powerful programs used to increase interactivity and functionality on Internet Web pages. ActiveX controls can also be misused to deliver service attacks, Trojans, droppers, and other similar malware. Unlike Java, ActiveX controls do not operate in a protected "sandbox" and can interact with the local drive, depending on permissions granted by the user!

HTML.   HyperText Markup Language, commonly referred to as HTML, is the foundation of Internet Web pages. While a few examples of HTML viruses have recently been discovered, the chances of getting a virus from HTML are basically nonexistent at the time of writing this book. However, integration of HTML with new functionality, such as ActiveX and JavaScript, may quickly change this situation.

A related bug in Windows 95/98 stems from malformed Internet links. When reserved and linked words are repeatedly used in a link, Windows 95/98 crashes. Calling certain DOS devices via an HTML link can also cause Windows 95/98 crashes. Used deliberately, these exploits can be used as a denial-of-service attack.

3

Myths and Hoaxes

Antivirus software developers have found that service calls from customers are regularly generated by viruses in the news and hoaxes circulated throughout the Internet. While it may be hard to believe, hoaxes often generate more service calls and online research from users than actual viruses. Hoaxes often warn of impending disaster on affected computers, raising the level of concern for the average user. This hoax method works extremely well, turning normal Internet users into e-mail spammers, sending the hoax message to everyone they know.

Myths

Fear is a growing problem in the computing industry, since the average user does not fully understand the technology and components of hardware and software systems. Clearly understanding the basics of computing goes a long way in differentiating between hoaxes, myths, and actual malware threats.

Capabilities of viruses

Viruses are not able to infect a system or carry out any malicious payload unless the user does something first. Common examples of risk-related activities include executing programs on a floppy disk, opening an e-mail attachment, and running a new download from the Internet.

Using programs like Outlook Express, which support auto-preview e-mail features, increases the risk of infection. Because auto-preview functions may be exploited by malware to infect a machine, it is best if users avoid using such features or use an e-mail program without such features.

The Media Are Not Always Accurate

Media reports written by individuals who are not experts in the field are sometimes inaccurate, skewed, or misleading. News reports about viruses often focus on what a virus *could* do rather than what is actually seen In the Wild. Another issue is the education of the reporters who write news media. For example, the word *virus* is often used to describe all types of malware, including Trojan horses and worms. Such subtle differences may dramatically affect the accuracy and impact of a news report.

Chernobyl is a good example of how media reports misidentify the capability of a virus to destroy hardware on a computer. Chernobyl, a variant of the CIH family, may damage instructions stored in flash BIOS and erase the contents of a drive, but it does not actually damage the hardware itself. Flash BIOS (firmware) damage can be prevented by using the motherboard to disable software changes to the BIOS. Repairing the flash BIOS and data on a drive can normally be done with software—no true hardware damage is present.

Antivirus companies have also played a role in fostering some of the fear and mystique regarding computer viruses and malware. Several companies have published news releases about a feature that offers protection against some sort of new virus technology that doesn't even exist In the Wild. Others have released reports about viruses that are well known in the field, but act as if they have discovered these viruses and as if they are high risks to users In the Wild. Such claims are often overexaggerated, designed to help sales of antivirus software. Fortunately there are companies and individuals within the industry that hold others accountable through the media, keeping such unethical practices down to a minimum.

To obtain a high-quality report, one must often refer to several online expert resources in the field of antivirus. Users also need to obtain a higher level of computing knowledge to understand the actual threats of new technologies such as Java and JavaScript.

Because most users don't have the time or interest to obtain such knowledge, it is important that they locate and regularly refer to expert resources that they can trust. Networking with a local IT representative in the company, finding a few expert resources online, and signing up for antivirus newsletters are all good examples of how a user can more easily stay informed without needing to have a deep understanding of antivirus technology.

Not all viruses are In the Wild

Reports about BubbleBoy were released to media worldwide. Many users were gravely concerned that they had been exposed to BubbleBoy, not realizing that it was only In the Zoo. While new malware exploiting such technology, such as Kak.Worm, has come out In the Wild at a later date, BubbleBoy was never a threat. Users had plenty of time to update security patches against the exploit before Kak.Worm was found In the Wild. Many media reports focus on what a virus can do rather than on the actual threat to users In the Wild.

Comments about BubbleBoy only existing In the Zoo were few and far between.

Not all viruses are widespread

Sometimes viruses are localized to an individual company or region of the world. For example, the Scores virus was developed by a disgruntled employee and released to a local company intranet. Early detection helped minimize the success of this virus In the Wild.

Other viral outbreaks are found more in specific regions of the world. For example, Chernobyl originally appeared in the United States, and several variants had been seen In the Wild before Chernobyl executed its deadly payload on April 26, 1999. As a result, U.S. users had a great deal of protection already in place because of the previous variants of Chernobyl seen In the Wild. At the same time, a large number of black market CD ROMs were sold in greater Asia, many with the Chernobyl virus. As many as 600,000 Asian users had their hard drives wiped out by the Chernobyl virus on April 26.

Other viruses are In the Wild but are rare. Rare viruses often are poor at replication or are easily detected by users or antivirus software. Often the most malicious viruses that people hear about, such as Hare, are promoted in the media but are never experienced by many individuals In the Wild. Many antivirus companies now rate the risk of infection when they announce a new virus found In the Wild. Ratings often change as events In the Wild change the risk of infection by a given virus. As outbreaks are discovered In the Wild, antivirus companies adjust the risk of infection accordingly.

Few viruses are malicious

A malicious virus is one that is specifically programmed to carry out a payload on a system that is malicious by intent. Unfortunately, many viruses are not designed to be malicious but still result in symptomatic damage or a major change in the operation of a computer.

As an example, if a virus runs in memory, it may conflict with legitimate programs run on the computer, sometimes crashing the computer. When the computer crashes, important files and data may be lost and hardware components may be damaged. While the virus was not designed to carry out such operations, the infection ultimately led to such a result.

At the time of the writing of this book, less than 10 percent of all viruses are designed to directly damage or delete software on a computer. Most of the media reports that the average user reads focus on viruses that are considered more newsworthy, the malicious viruses that wipe out hard drives and overwrite files. This is a natural phenomenon of news reporting and human nature—how many people want to read about another virus that doesn't do much besides replicate? It's only natural for people to focus on worst-case scenarios and events of great fear.

Some antivirus company reports of a new virus focus on the wrath of a new deadly payload but shy away from risk level. Unfortunately, many reports fail to mention that a virus is only In the Zoo or is so clunky in code that it has a poor replication and infection capability. Clearly presenting what matters most to users concerned about avoiding viruses is a conflict of interest for some antivirus software companies. At the same time, the media are more than happy to receive and publish such "newsworthy" reports to help boost their own sales and profit.

Few malicious viruses are widespread

Of the 10 percent or fewer of the viruses that are malicious, few are actually widespread In the Wild. Most malicious viruses are discovered In the Wild and then rarely seen after an initial outbreak. There are several factors that affect how well a malicious virus replicates In the Wild:

- The media get the word out, prompting some users to update antivirus programs immediately after a report of a malicious virus In the Wild.

- The effectiveness of the strategies employed by a virus to replicate varies.

- Some viruses delete themselves when they delete the contents of a drive, hampering replication efforts. The only hope for virus replication after executing such a payload is for the virus to have infected the contents of a different disk, such as a floppy or networked disk.

- Replication may be hampered by extra lines of code used for malicious purposes.

- Virus-specific programs are often created for more widespread programs, making it easy for some users to make sure they have identified and removed any such virus from a system.

- If a virus immediately executes a malicious payload, the user immediately detects the virus and takes actions to remove it from the system, hampering replication efforts.

Reading e-mail does not infect a computer

Recent security exploits from BubbleBoy technology and Kak.Worm have confused many users about the actual threat from reading e-mail. Just reading e-mail, with no bells and whistles, does not present a threat at this time.

Users of Microsoft Outlook and Outlook Express are exposed to a security hole surrounding auto-preview and Internet Explorer. Most users of Outlook programs have auto-preview enabled so that they can read e-mail by simply clicking on a message in the box of

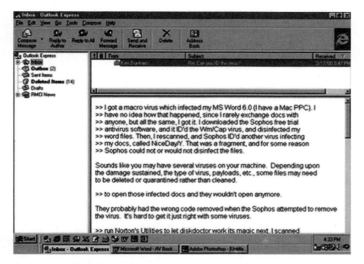

Figure 3.1 Outlook auto-preview.

interest. The e-mail clicked upon is promptly displayed, via auto-preview, in a separate pane below the e-mail box window. Figure 3.1 shows an Outlook Express window using auto-preview to view an e-mail message.

Worms like Kak.Worm exploit Internet Explorer, the auto-preview function of Outlook, to drop a script into the startup directory on the computer. After the computer is started up, a special script is run that infects the system. To avoid such malware, users of Outlook should disable auto-preview features and update Internet Explorer. Fortunately, such threats are still relatively rare In the Wild at this time.

Perhaps the greatest threat of replication In the Wild today are e-mail attachments. Users regularly share programs, Word documents, and other files with one another via e-mail. For many corporations, e-mail attachments are an essential communication tool. Opening attachments does put a computer at risk and should be done only after considering the risk, having updated antivirus software and other protection installed, and making backups on a regular basis.

All users should also make sure that related security threats, such as the Eyelet security hole in Microsoft Internet Explorer, are updated and patched as they are identified In the Wild. Having all programs regularly updated and patched is an important element of protection against new malware In the Wild. Make sure all updates are obtained from official, reputable sources on the Internet to avoid downloading a malware package disguised as a legitimate update file.

Virus Hoaxes

E-mail hoaxes are becoming one of the top concerns and reported incidences on the Internet today. As a rule of thumb, users should not believe unsolicited e-mail, especially chain letters. It's much like junk mail through regular postal mail. Why do some individuals believe that they have actually won the million dollars in the sweepstakes? It often comes down to hopes, dreams, ignorance, and fear.

When scrutinizing an unsolicited e-mail, the precept needs to be a lack of trust in what is written—even if it claims to be reported by an official source such as IBM. Simply checking out the facts on reputable Internet sites will quickly clarify most questions regarding the legitimacy of a virus warning.

Origin of hoaxes

Hoaxes and practical jokes have been around longer than computers. More recently, the Internet has enabled millions of users worldwide to communicate with one another more easily through a point-and-click interface. Growth of the Internet and e-mail services has skyrocketed in the last few years. The Internet now has more novice computer users than ever before. This new environment has resulted in a wide variety of new threats and hoaxes.

Perhaps the best-known e-mail hoax is Good Times, originally discovered In the Wild in 1994. Many hoaxes, including PenPal and Deeyenda, are variants within the Good Times family of hoaxes. The basic idea is that an authoritative source is warning users not to read e-mail, pending disaster, and asking users to send the notice to everyone they know—and they do!

While new security threats, such as Kak.Worm (BubbleBoy technology), are exploiting e-mail programs that use auto-preview functions, simply reading an e-mail is still relatively safe at this point in time. E-mail attachments and automated function and security exploits are the real threats In the Wild.

Identifying hoaxes

Most hoaxes have the following characteristics:

- The source of the e-mail is unreliable and/or unknown to the recipient.
- They refer to official sources and are written to sound official.
- They warn of tragic consequences, raising the level of concern.
- They warn of malware destroying hardware.
- They play upon the fears of most individuals, sometimes referring to new technology that is not well understood.
- They claim to be discussing malware that is new and unknown to researchers and antivirus software, with no known detection, repair, or removal tool currently available.
- They are posted in a newsgroup or area online that has nothing to do with viruses.
- They have spelling and grammatical mistakes.
- They are self-contradictory.
- They include a request to send the e-mail to everyone the reader knows rather than going to an Internet address that could be verified and reviewed.

While not every hoax contains these characteristics, they are seen in most e-mail hoaxes. Verify warnings with reputable sites online such as About.com Antivirus Software, About.com Urban Legends, Kumite.com, Virus Bulletin, CERT, Trend Micro, F-Secure, Symantec, McAfee, Sophos, and others.

If you don't see a warning posted online, check another source. Sometimes one site will have information on a new hoax or virus while another will have nothing listed.

If you search several sites and find nothing, then try forwarding your e-mail warning to an expert for analysis. One site, Hoax Kill at http://www.hoaxkill.com/hoaxes.html, lists common hoaxes and offers a warning service via e-mail. Simply e-mail hoaxes to hoaxkill@hoaxkill.com. Hoax Kill then contacts all previous e-mail recipients of the hoax message to educate/warn them about the hoax.

Another interesting twist, seen more recently In the Wild, is for an e-mail hoax to become a true threat. For example, the original Funprog.exe hoax warned users of the Chernobyl virus being transferred with Funprog.exe. While Chernobyl was prevalent In the Wild at the time, the original message was a hoax—there was no Chernobyl virus attached to Funprog.exe. A few days later, an individual with Chernobyl on the computer ran Funprog.exe, infecting it with Chernobyl, and then passed it on to a friend. Any time an e-mail hoax discusses something like a virus with an attachment, it could become real or closely resemble a true threat In the Wild.

E-mail Hoaxes In the Wild

Familiarize yourself with hoaxes In the Wild to gain a better understanding of e-mail hoaxes. Look for the common characteristics previously identified. The original formatting and spelling of hoax messages are given in Table 3.1. Hoaxes with several variants within a family are separated by dashes within the description field.

TABLE 3.1
E-mail Hoaxes

E-mail hoax	Description
A.I.D.S.	There is a virus out now being sent to people via email...it is called the A.I.D.S. VIRUS. It will destroy your memory, sound card and speakers, hard drive and it will infect your mouse or pointing device...as well as your keyboards making what you type not able to register on the screen. It self terminates only after it eats 5MB of hard drive space & will delete all programs.
	It will come via E-mail called "OPEN: VERY COOL! :)". Unless you configure your email program to launch attachments automatically, merely opening a message can't hurt you.
	Delete it immediately!! It will basically render your computer useless.
	PASS IT ON QUICKLY & TO AS MANY PEOPLE AS POSSIBLE!! THANKS!!
AOL4FREE.com (often confused with real AOL Trojan)	Anyone who recieves this must send it to as many people as you can. It is essential that this problem be reconciled as soon as possible.
	A few hours ago, I opened an E-mail that had the subject heading of aol4free.com.
	Within seconds of opening it, a window appeared and began to display my files that were being deleted. I immediately shut down my computer, but it was too late. This virus wiped me out.
	It ate the Anti-Virus Software that comes with the Windows '95 Program along with F-Prot AVS. Neither was able to detect it. Please be careful and send this to as many people as possible, so maybe this new virus can be eliminated.
Bad Times *A joke in light of those that believe in hoaxes.*	If you receive an email with a subject line of "Badtimes," delete it immediately WITH-OUT reading it. This is the most dangerous email virus yet. It will rewrite your hard

(Continued)

TABLE 3.1
E-mail Hoaxes (Continued)

E-mail hoax	Description
	drive. Not only that, but it will scramble any disks that are even close to your computer. It will recalibrate your refrigerator's coolness setting so that all your ice cream melts and milk curdles. It will demagnetize the strips on all your credit cards, reprogram your ATM access code, screw up the tracking on your VCR and use subspace field harmonics to scratch any CDs you try to play.
	It will give your ex-boy/girlfriend your new phone number. It will mix antifreeze into your fish tank. It will drink all your beer and leave its dirty socks on the coffee table when there's company coming over. It will hide your card keys when you are late for work and interfere with your car radio so that you hear only static while stuck in traffic. ...(Offensive material deleted)... It will replace your shampoo with Nair and your Nair with Rogaine, all while dating your current boy/girlfriend behind your back and billing their hotel rendezvous to your Visa card.
	Badtimes will give you Dutch Elm disease. It will leave the toilet seat up and leave the hair dryer plugged in dangerously close to a full bathtub. It will want only remove the forbidden tags from your mattresses and pillows, and refill your skim milk with whole. It is insidious and subtle. It is dangerous and terrifying to behold. It is also a rather interesting shade of mauve.These are just a few signs. Be very, very afraid.
Bud Frogs	DANGER! VIRUS ALERT!
	THIS IS A NEW TWIST. SOME CREEPOID SCAM-ARTIST IS SENDING OUT A VERY DESIRABLE SCREEN-SAVER {{THE BUD FROGS}}. IF YOU DOWN-LOAD IT, YOU'LL LOSE EVERYTHING!!!! YOUR HARD DRIVE WILL > CRASH!!

TABLE 3.1
E-mail Hoaxes (Continued)

E-mail hoax	Description
	DON'T DOWNLOAD THIS UNDER ANY CIRCUMSTANCES!!! IT JUST WENT INTO CIRCULATION ON 05/13/97, AS FAR AS I KNOW!! PLEASE DISTRIBUTE THIS WARNING TO AS MANY PEOPLE AS POSSIBLE...
	Someone is sending out a very cute screensaver of the Budweiser Frogs. If you download it, you will lose everything! Your hard drive will crash and someone from the Internet will get your screen name and password! DO NOT DOWNLOAD IT UNDER ANY CIRCUMSTANCES! It just went into circulation yesterday, as far as we know. Please distribute this message. This is a new, very malicious virus and not many people know about it. This information was announced yesterday morning from Microsoft.
	Please share it with everyone that might access the Internet. Once again, pass this along to EVERYONE in your address book so that this may be stopped. AOL has said this is a very dangerous virus and that there is NO remedy for it at this time. Please practice cautionary measures and forward this to all your on-line friend.
Deeyenda	There is a computer virus that is being sent across the Internet. If you receive an email message with the subject line "Deeyenda", DO NOT read the message, DELETE it immediately.
	It even goes so far as to claim the warning is from the FCC (as does the Good Times hoax). Further, the message claims that this "[virus] rewrites your hard drive, obliterating anything on it."
	Please ignore any messages regarding this supposed "virus" and do not pass on any messages regarding it. Passing on messages about this hoax serves only to further propagate it.

(Continued)

TABLE 3.1
E-mail Hoaxes (Continued)

E-mail hoax	Description
Elfbowl-Frogapult	IF YOU HAVE RECEIVED ANY OF THESE GAMES = FROGAPULT.EXE > > > > > ELFBOWL.EXE > > > > > (FROG GAME) & (ELF BOWLING GAME).
	PLEASE CAN YOU DELETE THEM COMPLETELY OUT OF YOUR SYSTEM AS THEY BOTH HAVE A DELAYED VIRUS ATTACHED TO THEM THAT WILL BE ACTIVATED ON CHRISTMAS DAY AND WILL WIPE OUT YOUR SYSTEM. LET EVERYONE KNOW OF THIS.
	————————
	Please Read!!
	Make sure if you sent this to anyone to delete this from your sent file and deleted files if your email is not set up to delete when you exit e-mail
	If you have received Elf Bowling or Frogapult games that have been circulating the internet, or know anyone who has, THEY MUST BE DELETED before Christmas day. THEY CONTAIN VIRUSES THAT ARE SET TO GO OFF ON CHRISTMAS DAY AND WILL DELETE YOUR HARD DRIVE.
	If you don't believe me, just wait and see. Our IT guy here just tested it on a non-networked PC, and everything was wiped out. Make certain that every copy is off of your hard drive or any servers. Please spread the word. These games are very detrimental to your computing life.
	——————————-
	Subject: FYI
	From a very reliable source, here is some documentation that we might Want to pass on:
	If you have received Elf Bowling or Frogapult games that have been circulating the Internet, or know anyone who has, they MUST BE DELETED before Christmas day.

TABLE 3.1
E-mail Hoaxes (Continued)

E-mail hoax	Description
	THEY CONTAIN VIRUSES THAT ARE SET TO GO OFF ON CHRISTMAS DAY AND WILL DELETE YOUR HARD DRIVE.
	If you don't believe me, just wait and see. Our IT guy here just tested it on a non-networked PC, and everything was wiped out. Make certain that every copy is off of your hard drive or any servers. Please spread the word. These games are very detrimental to your computing life.
Funprog.exe	This is extremely important. There is an exec file going around called "Funprog.exe" and it contains the CIH virus. If you receive it, DO NOT DOWNLOAD IT.
	But here is the worst part of it. This virus is being sent out from names you know. Somehow they found a way to use other peoples screen names and send out mail. If you are an AOL user and you get mail from anyone on AOL including me that says @aol.com after the screen name DO NOT DOWNLOAD that piece of mail. It will not be from that person that you think is sending it to you.
	AOL is very aware of what is going on right now. Please do not download anything. I rather all of us be safe than sorry, until AOL fixes this problem.
	For example, the mail would look like this:
	Subj: EXEC Warning Date: 10/03/1999 8:12:13 PM Eastern Daylight Time From: *Omitted*
	My mail would never say "@aol.com" since I am an AOL member...thats the give away! Please forward this letter to all your friends...
Geschenk (joke program—not a virus)	I received a forward this morning from a friend with a neat little thing attached called "Gift.EXE." I ran it, and assumed that

(Continued)

TABLE 3.1
E-mail Hoaxes (Continued)

E-mail hoax	Description
	it was clean, since Norton Antivirus said it was okay. It wasn't. I sent a copy to a friend of mine that just so happens to work at a software company, and low and behold, it had a virus: Found virus JOKE_GESCHENK in file Gift.exe
	I ran it, and it has a red screen with tiny Coca-Cola logos on it, and says something about being a great customer, and giving the gift of a free drink holder. At that point, it kicks open your CD-ROM. Great joke, but you don't find out right away that your computer is INFECTED!!!
Good Times	Here is some important information. Beware of a file called Goodtimes.
	Happy Chanukah everyone, and be careful out there. There is a virus on America Online being sent by E-Mail. If you get anything called "Good Times", DON'T read it or download it. It is a virus that will erase your hard drive. Forward this to all your friends. It may help them a lot.
	Soon after the release of CIAC NOTES 04, another "Good Times" message was circulated. This is the same message that is being circulated during this recent "Good Times" rebirth. This message includes a claim that the Federal Communications Commission (FCC) released a warning about the danger of the "Good Times" virus. This "Good Times" hoax message contains the following:
	The FCC released a warning last Wednesday concerning a matter of major importance to any regular user of the InterNet. Apparently, a new computer virus has been engineered by a user of America Online that is unparalleled in its destructive capability. Other, more well-known viruses such as Stoned, Airwolf, and Michaelangelo pale in comparison to the prospects of this newest creation by a warped mentality.

TABLE 3.1
E-mail Hoaxes (Continued)

E-mail hoax	Description
	What makes this virus so terrifying, said the FCC, is the fact that no program needs to be exchanged for a new computer to be infected.
	——————————
	PLEASE READ THE MESSAGE BELOW !!!!!!!!!!!!!
	Some miscreant is sending email under the title "Good Times" nationwide, if you get anything like this, DON'T DOWN LOAD THE FILE!
	It has a virus that rewrites your hard drive, obliterating anything t. Please be careful and forward this mail to anyone you care about. The FCC released a warning last Wednesday concerning a matter of major importance to any regular user of the Internet. Apparently a new computer virus has been engineered by a user of AMERICA ON LINE that is unparalleled in its destructive capability. Other more well-known viruses such as "Stoned", "Airwolf" and "Michaelangelo" pale in comparison to the prospects of this newest creation by a warped mentality. What makes this virus so terrifying, said the FCC, is the fact that no program needs to be exchanged for a new computer to be infected. It can be spread through the existing email systems of the Internet.
	Once a Computer is infected, one of several things can happen. If the computer contains a hard drive, that will most likely be destroyed. If the program is not stopped, the computer's processor will be placed in an nth-complexity infinite binary loop -which can severely damage the processor if left running that way too long. Unfortunately, most novice computer users will not realize what is happening until it is far too late. Luckily, there is one sure means of detecting what is now known as the "Good Times" virus. It always travels to new computers the same way in a text email message with the subject line reading "Good Times".

(*Continued*)

TABLE 3.1
E-mail Hoaxes (Continued)

E-mail hoax	Description
	Avoiding infection is easy once the file has been received simply by NOT READING IT! The act of loading the file into the mail server's ASCII buffer causes the "Good Times" mainline program to initialize and execute.
	The program is highly intelligent—it will send copies of itself to everyone whose email address is contained in a receive-mail file or a sent-mail file, if it can find one. It will then proceed to trash the computer it is running on.
	The bottom line is:—if you receive a file with the subject line "Good Times", delete it immediately! Do not read it" Rest assured that whoever's name was on the "From" line was surely struck by the virus. Warn your friends and local system users of this newest threat to the Internet! It could save them a lot of time and money.
	Could you pass this along to your global mailing list as well?
	—————————
	********IMPORTANT*******
	PLEASE SEND TO PEOPLE YOU CARE ABOUT OR JUST PEOPLE ONLINE
Gullibility Virus *A joke in light of those that believe in hoaxes.*	WASHINGTON, D.C.-The Institute for the Investigation of irregular Internet Phenomena announced today that many Internet users are becoming infected by a new virus that causes them to believe without question every groundless story, legend, and dire warning that shows up in their Inbox or on their browser. The Gullibility Virus, as it is called, apparently makes people believe and forward copies of silly hoaxes relating to E-Mail viruses, get-rich-quick schemes, and conspiracy theories. "These are not just readers of tabloids or people who buy lottery tickets based on fortune cookie numbers," a spokesman said. "Most are

TABLE 3.1
E-mail Hoaxes (Continued)

E-mail hoax	Description
	otherwise normal people, who would laugh at the same stories if told to them by a stranger on a street corner."
	However, once these same people become infected with the Gullibility Virus, they believe anything they read on the Internet. "My immunity to tall tales and bizarre claims is all gone," reported one weeping victim. "I believe every warning message and sick child story my friends forward to me, even though most of the messages are anonymous."
	Internet users are urged to examine themselves for symptoms of the virus, which include the following
	■ the willingness to believe improbable stories without thinking ■ the urge to forward multiple copies of such stories to others ■ a lack of desire to take three minutes to check to see if a story is true
	T. C. is an example of someone recently infected. He told one reporter, "I read on the Net that the major ingredient in almost all shampoos makes your hair fall out, so I've stopped using shampoo." When told about the Gullibility Virus, T . C. said he would stop reading e-mail, so that he would not become infected. President Clinton has been advised by the National Health Council. He has had an emergency session with former presidents Bush, Reagan, Carter, Ford, and Lincoln. All agreed he should not quarantine the country.
	This is not being reported in the major news media to avoid panic. Anyone with symptoms is urged to seek help immediately. Experts recommend that at the first feelings of gullibility, Internet users rush to their favorite search engine and look up the item tempting them to thoughtless credence. Most hoaxes, legends, and tall tales have been

(Continued)

TABLE 3.1
E-mail Hoaxes (Continued)

E-mail hoax	Description
	widely discussed and exposed by the Internet community. Many companies have internal support groups to help employees minimize the impact of this terrible virus.
	***
	Forward this message to all your friends right away! Don't think about it! This is not a chain letter! This story is true! Don't check it out! This story is so timely, there is no date on it! This story is so important, we're using lots of exclamation points!!! For every message you forward to some unsuspecting person, the Home for the Hopelessly Gullible will donate ten cents to itself. (If you wonder how the Home will know you are forwarding these messages all over creation, you're obviously thinking too much).
How to Give a Cat a Colonic (See Wobbler for related variant)	If you receive an e-mail entitled, "How to Give a Cat a Colonic," DO NOT open it. It will erase everything on your hard drive. Forward this letter out to as many people as you can. This is a new, very malicious virus and not many people know about it. This information was announced by IBM.
	Please share it with everyone that might access the Internet. Once again, pass this along to EVERYONE in your address book so that this may be stopped. AOL has said that this is a very dangerous virus and that there is NO remedy for it at this time. Please practice cautionary measures and forward this to all your online friends ASAP.
	———————————
	To All with a Computer,
	PLEASE READ THE FOLLOWING CAREFULLY
	VIRUS WARNING a new Virus - WOBBLER is on the loose. It will arrive on e-mail titled "How to Give a Cat a Colonic". IBM

TABLE 3.1
E-mail Hoaxes (Continued)

E-mail hoax	Description
	and AOL have announced that it is very powerful, more so than melissa. There is no remedy. It will eat all your information on the hard drive and also destroys Netscape Navigator and Microsoft Internet Explorer. Do not open anything with this title and please pass this message on to all your contacts and anyone who uses your e-mail facility. Not many people seem to know about this yet so propagate it as fast as possible.
	This information was announced yesterday morning by IBM. Please share it with everyone in your address book so that the spreading of the virus may be stopped. This is a very dangerous Virus and there is no remedy for it at this time.
	Please practice cautionary measures and forward this to all your online friends A.S.A.P.
	Thank you!
It Takes Guts to Say Jesus!	If you receive an email titled "It Takes Guts to Say 'Jesus' " DO NOT open it. It will erase everything on your hard drive. Forward this letter out to as many people as you can. This is a new, very malicious virus and not many people know about it. This information was announced yesterday morning from IBM; please share it with everyone that might access the internet. Once again, pass this along to EVERYONE in your address book so that this may be stopped. Also, do not open or even look at any mail that says "RETURNED OR UNABLE TO DELIVER." This virus will attach itself to your computer components and render them useless. Immediately delete any mail items that say this. AOL has said that this is a very dangerous virus and that there is NO remedy for it at this time. Please practice cautionary measures and forward this to all your online friends ASAP.

(*Continued*)

TABLE 3.1
E-mail Hoaxes (Continued)

E-mail hoax	Description
	LeeAnn
	[*phone number*]
	————————
	A new variant has appeared in the wake of the Melissa virus:
	VIRUS WARNING:
	If you receive an email titled "It Takes Guts to Say 'Jesus' DO NOT OPEN IT. It will erase everything on your hard drive. This information was announced yesterday morning from IBM; AOL states that this is a very dangerous virus, much worse than "Melissa", and that there is NO remedy for it at this time.
	Some very sick individual has succeeded in using the reformat function from Norton Utilities causing it to completely erase all documents on the hard drive. It has been designed to work with Netscape Navigator and Microsoft Internet Explorer. It destroys Macintosh and IBM compatible computers.
	This is a new, very malicious virus and not many people know about it. Pass this warning along to EVERYONE in your address book and please share it with all your online friends ASAP so that this threat may be stopped.
	Please practice cautionary measures and tell anyone that may have access to your computer.
	Forward this warning to everyone that might access the Internet.
PenPal	If anyone receives mail entitled: PENPAL GREETINGS! please delete it WITHOUT reading it.
	This is a warning for all internet users— there is a dangerous virus propogating across the internet through an e-mail

TABLE 3.1
E-mail Hoaxes (Continued)

E-mail hoax	Description
	message entitled "PENPAL GREETINGS!". DO NOT DOWNLOAD ANY MESSAGE ENTITLED "PENPAL GREETINGS!" This message appears to be a friendly letter asking you if you are interested in a penpal, but by the time you read this letter, it is too late. The "trojan horse" virus will have already infected the boot sector of your hard drive, destroying all of the data present. It is a self-replicating virus, and once the message is read, it will AUTOMATICALLY forward itself to anyone who's e-mail address is present in YOUR mailbox!
	This virus will DESTROY your hard drive, and holds the potential to DESTROY the hard drive of anyone whose mail is in your inbox, and who's mail is in their inbox, and so on. If this virus remains unchecked, it has the potntial to do a great deal of DAMAGE to computer networks worldwide!!!!
	Please, delete the message entitled "PEN-PAL GREETINGS!" as soon as you see it! And pass this message along to all of your friends and relatives, and the other readers of the newsgroups and mailing lists which you are on, so that they are not hurt by this dangerous virus!!!!
Win a Holiday	If you receive an email titled "WIN A HOLI-DAY" DO NOT open it. It will erase everything on your hard drive. Forward this letter outto as many people as you can. This is a new, very malicious virus and not many people know about it. This information was announced yesterday (16/2/98) morning from Microsoft; please share it with everyone that might access the internet. Once again, pass this along to EVERYONE in your address book so that this may be stopped. Also, do not open or even look at any mail that says "RETURNED OR UNABLE TO DELIVER" This virus will attach itself to your computer components and render them useless.

(Continued)

TABLE 3.1
E-mail Hoaxes (Continued)

E-mail hoax	Description
	Immediately delete any mail items that say this. AOL has said that this is a very dangerous virus and that there is NO remedy for it at this time. Please practice cautionary measures and forward this to all your online friends = ASAP.
	Dangerous - Pls take note below:
	If you receive an e-mail titled "PLEASE HELP POOR DOG, Win A Holiday" DO NOT open it. It will erase everything on your hard drive. Forward this letter out to as many people as you can. This is a new, very malicious virus and not many people know about it. This was announced yesterday morning from Microsoft, please share it with everyone who might access the Internet.
Wobbler	WARNING: If you receive an e-mail with a file called California, do not open the file. The file contains the WOBBLER virus. This information was announced yesterday morning from IBM; AOL states that this is a very dangerous virus, much worse than "Melissa", and that there is NO remedy for it at this time.
	Some very sick individual has succeeded in using the reformat function from Norton Utilities causing it to completely erase all documents on the hard drive. It has been designed to work with Netscape Navigator and Microsoft Internet Explorer. It destroys Macintosh and IBM compatible computers. This is a new, very malicious virus and not many people know about it. Pass this warning along to EVERYONE in your address book ASAP so that this threat may be stopped.
	————————
	A serious virus warning folks. The following has been confirmed by F-Secure (Datafellows): A new virus—WOBBLER will be launched in 7 to 10 days time. It will coincide with

TABLE 3.1
E-mail Hoaxes (Continued)

E-mail hoax	Description
	some presidential happening in Los Angeles in the USA. It will arrive on an e-mail titled "CALIFORNIA". This virus is announced to be more powerful and destructive than MELISSA and of course there is NO REMEDY as yet.
	If you should open anything with title then kiss all your hard drive information good bye. It will also destroy Netscape Navigator and Internet Explorer.
	This information can be verified by AOL, IBM and Datafellows (old F-PROT).
	PLEASE TAKE THIS SERIOUSLY AND WARN AS MANY PEOPLE AS POSSIBLE.
	Have a nice day!
	—————————
	A new virus
	It will arrive on e-mail titled "CALIFORNIA". IBM and AOL have announced that it is VERY powerful, more so than Melissa, there is no remedy.
	It will EAT all your information on the hard drive and it also destroys Netscape Navigator and Microsoft Internet Explorer.
	Do not open anything with this title and please pass this message on to all your contacts and anyone who uses your e-mail facility. Not many people seem to know about this yet, so propagate it as fast as possible!
	—————————
	It will arrive on e-mail titled "How to Give a Cat a Colonic."
	CALIFORNIA IBM and AOL have announced that it is very powerful, more so than Melissa.
	There is no remedy.

(*Continued*)

TABLE 3.1
E-mail Hoaxes (Continued)

E-mail hoax	Description
	It will eat all your information on the hard drive and also destroys Netscape Navigator and Microsoft Internet Explorer. Do not open anything with this title and please pass this message on to all your contacts and anyone who uses your e-mail facility.
	Not many people seem to know about this yet so propagate it as fast as possible.
	This information was announced yesterday morning by IBM; please share it with everyone in your address book so that the spreading of the virus may be stopped.
	This is a very dangerous virus and there is no remedy for it at this time.
	VIRUS WARNING a new Virus—WOBBLER is on the loose. It will arrive on e-mail titled "How to Give a Cat a Colonic". IBM and AOL have announced that it is very powerful, more so than Melissa. There is no remedy.
	It will eat all your information on the hard drive and also destroys Netscape Navigator and Microsoft Internet Explorer. Do not open anything with this title and please pass this message on to all your contacts and anyone who uses your e-mail facility. Not many people seem to know about this yet so propagate it as fast as possible. This information was announced yesterday morning by IBM. Please share it with everyone in your address book so that the spreading of the virus may be stopped.
	This is a very dangerous Virus and there is no remedy for it at this time. Please practice cautionary measures and forward this to all your online friends A.S.A.P.
Y2KFIX.EXE	PLEASE READ AND SEND TO EVERYONE YOU KNOW!!
	Do Not Download: Y2KFIX.EXE ~~~~~It will come to you as....... "America Online

TABLE 3.1
E-mail Hoaxes (Continued)

E-mail hoax	Description
	Year 2000 Update" it will have a File: Y2KFIX.EXE (41229 bytes) DL Time (115200 bps): 1 minute
	DO NOT DOWNLOAD IT, ITS A VIRUS .
	1) IF AOL WANTED TO UPDATE YOUR SYSTEM, THEY WOULD DO IT WHILE YOU WERE ONLINE, NOT THIS WAY
	2) IF AOL WERE TO DO IT THIS WAY THEY WOULD JUST SEND YOU AN EMAIL TO CONTACT THEIR WEBSIGHT AND THEN DOWNLOAD THE NECES-SARY FILE
	FORWARD TO "TOSEMAIL1" THE REST OF IT GOES AS FOLLOWS:
	Hello, I am *name omitted* of the AOL TECH Team and we have recently finished work on this project which is the AOL Year 2000 Update. The function of this program is to make your AOL version completely compatible with the year 2000 bugs that will occur on most computers. This program will work on Windows 3.1, Windows 95, Windows 98, and Macintosh. It has been made to be as user-friendly as possible. You just have to: 1. Double click on the icon 2. Restart your computer and your computer and AOL will automatically be updated. If you experience any problems with this file please report them to this e-mail address.
	Thanks for your time,
	NAME
	AOL Tech Staf

See the "Identifying Hoaxes Lesson Plan" in Appendix E to learn more about how to distinguish between viruses and hoaxes.

4

Detecting Malware

The first goal of any successful antivirus program is to detect malware before it gets a chance to enter or infect a system. If an antivirus program misses even one virus, it could spell disaster; 100 percent detection is required for complete protection. Unfortunately, new malware and their variants often bypass complex antivirus detection strategies. One must strive for reasonable protection, rather than complete protection, often using more than one antivirus program to decrease the risk of infection.

Symptoms of Infection

Malware infections often display a wide variety of symptoms that are confused with normal computer operations and malfunctions. Updated antivirus software should always be installed and running on a machine with an on-access scanner running. Consider running a manual scan to reasonably rule out virus infections when troubleshooting a problem on a computer.

Table 4.1 outlines symptoms of infection and how viruses may cause such results.

TABLE 4.1
Virus Symptoms

Symptoms	How Viruses Cause Symptom
Delayed startup, processing, or loading of files and programs.	Viruses running in memory may inadvertently slow down normal processes on the infected computer.
Windows 32-bit disk can't be used during startup error message.	Error messages about the startup disk may indicate a boot sector virus infection.
Increase in program file size.	When a virus infects a program, it parasitically attaches virus code to existing program code, normally increasing file size.
Disk runs out of free space.	Every virus infection normally increases the file size of the infected program. A computer can become severely infected, with virus code taking up a large majority of space on the drive. More often, users merely have limited drive space available and may need to defragment and run Scan Disk or optimize the desktop (Macintosh) to free up available space on a drive.
CHKDSK doesn't show 655360 bytes available.	Some virus infections may change the value of total bytes available, reported by CHKDSK. Legitimate programs may also change this value.
Unexpected errors.	Viruses that run in memory or affect system files may result in errors and faults. Accidental conflicts between viruses and legitimate programs on a computer are a common side effect of virus infections. For example, Trojan infections sometimes result in 216 Runtime errors, such as "Runtime Error 216 at 00002021."
Drive light flashes when user isn't doing anything.	Viruses running in memory may be accessing the drive to infect files, even when a user isn't using any software. It may also be a legitimate program, such as antivirus software or FastFind, running in the background.
Can't access the hard drive when booting from a floppy disk.	When booting from a floppy disk, some viruses attempt to limit access to the hard drive. Scanning the Master Boot

TABLE 4.1
Virus Symptoms (Continued)

Symptoms	How Viruses Cause Symptom
	Record for viruses, after booting from a known clean floppy, is a good troubleshooting step. Legitimate access issues may arise with NTFS and FAT32 partitioned disks.
New files, file names, file dates, or file times found on drive.	New and modified files are sometimes created by malware upon infection. Backup questionable files to a floppy disk, drag the file to the recycle bin, restart, and test functionality. If the file is needed to run a program, simply open the recycle bin and right-click on the file of interest to Restore it to the original location; restart and test functionality again. If the file is not needed, empty the recycle bin after a few days or save a copy to a floppy disk and delete it immediately from the hard drive.
My friends are getting e-mails from me that I didn't send.	Some malware, such as Happy99.exe (SKA), uses the address book of e-mail programs to send messages and malware to other computers. If friends complain about getting messages from you that you didn't send, it's time to scan for viruses with updated software to rule out worms, Trojans, and other exploits.
Clicking noises or music is played on the computer.	Some viruses, such as Form, have a payload that sometimes plays a clicking noise or musical tune each time a key is pressed. Audio feedback is also a legitimate feature of programs and operating systems.
I have to change the date on the computer each time I start up.	The battery inside the computer may need to be replaced or a virus may be affecting the date setting on the computer.
Low memory.	If a virus is running in memory, it may cause low memory situations to arise on a computer with limited RAM.
Bad sectors on floppy or disk errors.	Disk errors may occur for a variety of reasons, including static electricity.

(Continued)

TABLE 4.1
Virus Symptoms (Continued)

Symptoms	How Viruses Cause Symptom
	Viruses may also cause such a report, sometimes attempting to use certain blocks on a disk to store virus data.
Files on the drive are erased or damaged.	Viruses like Chernobyl attempt to erase the contents of the hard drive on infected computers. Drive contents may be erased for a variety of reasons, but are often related to viruses if not initiated by the user through troubleshooting or system setup.
Word files contain macros.	Microsoft Word programs may contain macros for a variety of functions. If Microsoft Word macro protection is enabled, users will be warned of documents containing macros before they are enabled. Most users simply disable and avoid the use of macros in Word to lower the risk of infection. Macros may also be a legitimate tool of a Microsoft Word document that is completely free of viruses.
Code shows up in a file I'm authoring, and I didn't create it.	If programming in a program such as FrontPage, some code may be automatically generated by the software tools. It's also possible that a virus inserts code that you now see because of your editing of a given file recently infected by a virus.
Unusual uploading activity.	Malware may be uploading data from the infected computer if large amounts of data are uploaded while online. Monitoring such behavior may help detect a password-stealing Trojan. Legitimate reasons include user-initiated uploads, registration of software, and use of interactive Internet games.
Unable to save or open a document.	Some Microsoft Word viruses disable the ability for a user to save, open, or perform other common operations from within Word. Legitimate reasons may include lack of user knowledge regarding the program in use or limitations set by programs to work in various modes of operation, such as graphics versus text.

TABLE 4.1
Virus Symptoms (Continued)

Symptoms	How Viruses Cause Symptom
Strange picture or messages appear on the screen.	Viruses, such as Class, display messages that often prompt users to install and run updated antivirus software. Other malware, such as Happy99.exe (SKA), uses visual payloads more like a Trojan, to infect the computer while the user watches a fireworks animation. Other programs may contain an unusual screen as part of the program, inadvertently raising the level of concern for some users.
Antivirus software detects a virus.	Antivirus programs identify viruses under a variety of names. Sometimes a legitimate file or string of code is misidentified as a virus, resulting in a false alarm. Scanning with more than one on-demand antivirus program provides better protection and support for questionable reports.
Computer crashes.	Bugs in software, more often the case, crash a computer. Newer forms of malware, including Java applets and JavaScript, may attempt to close a program or crash a computer. Viruses running in memory may accidentally crash a computer.
File becomes password protected or password is changed.	Some viruses, such as password, may add or change a password on a document or program.

Unfortunately, viruses are more commonly identified on a system by ruling out a virus infection and knowing what is not a virus. If antivirus software has not been operating on a machine suspected of containing a virus infection, boot from a clean, locked floppy disk and scan for viruses on the computer using updated antivirus software. This reasonably rules out a virus infection on a system.

Antivirus Software Scanning Methods

Antivirus software programs support a wide range of scanning methods and operating environments. Each scanning method supports a unique technique for preventing, detecting, and removing malware from the system.

Scanning during startup and shutdown

Scanning during startup and shutdown helps antivirus programs to detect and remove viruses that may have entered the system during operation or a recent startup effort. For example, Master Boot Record (MBR) viruses infect the hard drive when a computer is booted from an infected floppy disk. MBR viruses often exploit user habits, where a user leaves an infected disk in the drive during shutdown. When the computer is started up the MBR-virus-infected floppy is run, infecting the hard drive.

Shutdown scans not only scan for viruses on the system but may also prompt the user to remove any disks detected on the system. This helps lower the risk of MBR infections with future startups and also helps users secure floppy disks that may otherwise have been inadvertently left in the computer.

On-access scanning

All leading commercial packages include an on-access scanner that helps to protect against viruses while the computer is in use. On-access scanners monitor system activity and scan files and programs as they are opened. As a general rule, on-access scanners are not as robust as manual scans initiated by a user with an on-demand program. Nevertheless, on-access scanners are an important element of every antivirus program.

Although on-access scanners only take up a small amount of available memory, they can cause noticeable performance issues on older and more limited computers. To help minimize performance issues most default settings for on-access scanners are set to "Programs only" by antivirus setup programs. Unfortunately that puts the computer at risk for viruses that do not infect programs, giving users a false sense of security. For serious antivirus protection, users should modify on-access preferences to scan all types of files and programs.

Using two antivirus programs on a computer is highly recommended, but not two on-access scanners. On-access scanners more often compete with one another and negatively impact system performance. One on-access scanner from a robust program, set to scan all files, is a reasonable measure of protection. Manually initiate scans from the second program, periodically, to double-check a system.

Baiting and waiting

A "bait-and-wait" method can be used to detect and analyze viruses on a system. Bait-and-wait files fall under a host of names, including bait files, decoy files, victim files, and goat files. The idea is that a file is created by an antivirus program to lie in wait of an infection. When changes occur to the file, the antivirus program takes appropriate action to detect and remove the offending malware. This method is most often used by antivirus researchers to create a simple file to be infected, making disassembly of an infected document a much clearer and easier process.

Self-scans

Some viruses attempt to remain undetected by specifically infecting antivirus programs. Similar to on-access scanners, some viruses work to intercept antivirus scanning and detection. Most antivirus programs currently scan themselves for a virus to avoid being partially disabled by such a virus.

Antivirus Software Detection Methods

Search string updates

Traditional antivirus programs rely heavily upon a database of virus search strings to detect viruses on a computer. Although developers use a variety of names for this type of database, such as signature file, pattern file, and DAT file, they all provide the same type of functionality to an antivirus program. When an antivirus program scans a file, it compares data in the scanned file with data in the search strings database. If a reasonable match is found, a virus is considered to be in the file being scanned.

The obvious weak point of such a methodology is that viruses not found in the search strings database may easily escape detection from the antivirus program. Another weak point is how often the search strings database is updated. Many users only update monthly, if at all, leaving their computer exposed to potentially hundreds of new viruses each month. This risk becomes increasingly important when a new malicious virus, such as Chernobyl in 1999, is found In the Wild. If the search strings database is not updated, such a virus may go undetected, wreaking havoc on a system when the payload is executed.

How a search string database is updated also makes a difference. Some companies upgrade an entire package each month, while offering updates to the search string database on an as-needed basis for malware discovered In the Wild. Others offer updates to a search string database on a less frequent basis.

One of the most common problems associated with new computer owners is the installation of bundled software on the computer. Because the software comes installed on the new computer, the new user assumes that it is updated and working properly. Unfortunately, most computer manufacturers install software from image files that are often several months old. The result is that many new computer users end up relying upon software with signature files that are severely outdated. More often than not, new computer users find this out the hard way—after a virus infection occurs.

File size change

Antivirus programs use the checksum method to run an initial scan on files to calculate a checksum value. Any change in the checksum value may indicate a virus infection. When a virus infects a file, it attaches itself parasitically to an existing program, often increasing the file size of the infected program.

Viruses often attempt to minimize detection by keeping file size changes to a minimum. Cavity viruses, such as Lehigh, are an extreme example, where a virus overwrites code in an existing program with new virus code. If successful, the cavity virus does not affect functionality of the infected program or file size. Several antivirus programs look for changes to any file, helping to identify viruses that do not change the file size of a program.

One of the complications for this method of virus detection is that program files are often legitimately increased by the user. Installing a patch update, running a setup program, using editing features within a program, or editing the code of a program are all common actions that are not viral. This is one reason why search string databases are so important to antivirus programs—they compare changes made to a program to known virus strings. A future challenge for antivirus programs is to automatically discern between legitimate changes and virus infections.

CHKDSK file size change

A traditional, but somewhat outdated, technique is to check the available memory reported by CHKDSK to see if it reads 655360 bytes available. If not, a virus may have infected the program or a legitimate program may have changed the reported amount available. CHKDSK is only one of several checks that a user might use to manually identify an infected system.

Changes to `normal.dot`

`Normal.dot`, `normal` on a Macintosh, is a Microsoft Word file that is normally opened each time Microsoft Word is launched. A common method for macro virus infection is to infect `normal.dot` with a virus. This enables the virus to load into memory each time Microsoft Word is run. Macros running in memory work to carry out payloads and spread to other documents on the infected computer.

Heuristic detection

Heuristic technology, a big part of commercial antivirus programs today, look for "viruslike" code in an attempt to identify new or previously undiscovered viruses In the Wild. Although exact matches of virus strings are easy to identify, simple variants can go undetected. Heuristics go beyond exact matches, looking in as many ways as possible to identify new variants of a family as well as new viruses In the Wild.

Heuristics have traditionally been underutilized by users of antivirus software. Most heuristic settings are set to medium or low to avoid large amounts of false alarms (false positive/flag), where viruslike code turns out to be normal software. Changing the sensitivity of heuristic scans to high has historically resulted in an almost unusable antivirus scanner for some computers, prompting the user to check various files on an all-too-frequent basis. The result is that heuristic technology misses new viruses In the Wild because it is difficult to use and doesn't have the capabilities to easily distinguish viruslike code from actual virus code. Fortunately, antivirus developers have improved heuristic code to be more user friendly and useful in the last few years.

Behavioral analysis

Some developers, such as InDefense, are taking a rather bold and progressive approach toward fighting off viruses, behavioral analysis. Rather than relying on a signature file database of known viruses, InDefense works to proactively protect the system by carefully monitoring the behavior of the system. Detailed snapshots of the system are taken so that any attempted change may be carefully analyzed for malicious activity. The whole idea is to prevent virus infections before they occur.

Although some scoff at the idea, it's hard to ignore the success of InDefense, certified by West Coast Labs as a Level 1 certified program, able to detect 100 percent of all viruses In the Wild. Such programs, working to identify and block malware before an infection occurs, offer great promise.

Port monitoring.   Expert users may want to monitor ports in an effort to identify an infection on a system, especially from malware such as Trojans that make use of Remote Access Tools. A variety of programs, such as X-NetStat and Trojan Defence Suite (TDS), are available to expert PC users to monitor ports. Users of Windows may use the MS-DOS Prompt to enter `netstat  help` in DOS to learn how to use NetStat to check the status of a system. Using commands such as `NETSTAT  -A  -N` will list all connections and listening ports in numerical order.

Submitting Suspicious Files

Many virus experts gladly accept user-submitted files for analysis to determine if someone has contracted a computer virus or other type of malware. Make sure that you've scanned the computer with updated antivirus software in a controlled environment (from a clean floppy disk) before submitting a virus to an expert for review. Then document the following details:

- Date and location of suspected infection.

- Name of virus if virus family or variant is known. Include as much text related to the virus as possible, since viruses fall under a variety of names.

- Type of computer, version and type of operating system, memory, and configuration if known. The more details that you can provide, the more a researcher has to work with when analyzing a sample.

- Antivirus and other software on the system, including versions. Use more than one on-demand scanner to detect and remove malware before submitting a sample.

- Report and log files provided by antivirus software on the system.

- Symptoms of infection.

- Recent changes made on the system.

- Troubleshooting steps taken to date.

Many commercial programs are now automating submissions, sending files to an antivirus laboratory immediately after detection on an intranet. In contrast, depending upon the type of virus that has infected the computer, sending a virus sample manually can be somewhat challenging.

Capturing viruses for analysis

To capture a virus, copy a variety of files to a floppy disk. What you copy depends upon what type of virus you think you have. Start by formatting a floppy disk to send to a virus expert for analysis. If a Master Boot Record virus is on the hard drive, it may infect the floppy disk during reformatting.

After formatting a disk, restart Windows in DOS mode by pressing F8 during startup. At the DOS prompt type C:\Windows\System to navigate to the system folder on the C drive. Then use the copy command to copy the following files (example: `copy command.com a:`).

- `Command.com`
- `Debug.exe`
- `Edit.com`
- `Fdisk.exe`
- `Format.com`
- `Himem.sys`
- `Setver.exe`
- `Win.com`
- `NotePad.exe`
- `Taskman.exe`

To capture Microsoft Word macro viruses, also copy the following files to a floppy disk:

- `Normal.dot`, located in the Templates folder of Microsoft Office
- The Microsoft Word file in question
- Any other template or file that is in question

To capture Excel-based viruses copy over any Excel file in question, `.XLA`, and `.XLS` files in question. If applications appear to be infected, copy over to disk smaller applications. Trojans and worms are easily copied to a disk, just like an infected program.

5

Preventative Measures

According to the ICSA.net Labs 1999 Computer Virus Prevalence Survey, 55 percent of surveyed organizations reported having antivirus software installed on all computers in the workplace. Only 60 percent of all computers reported on used full-time, automatic, on-access antivirus software. Even more alarming, most respondents reported having few if any network protections in place, such as firewalls, proxy servers, or e-mail scanning.

Such reports are alarming when antivirus protection options are so readily available and affordable for both home and corporate environments. Viruses continue to be a problem because of a lack of preventative measures, poor installations, and maintenance of antivirus solutions, and new exploits In the Wild.

Preventative measures are the key to success in the antivirus world. It's too late to back up files after a malicious virus outbreak. Employees have already lost precious time and resources after a computer is disrupted by a virus infection. Simply reacting to viruses—not planning ahead—is a bad idea, and can be very costly.

The expense of a malware outbreak within an organization is not limited to loss of data alone. A variety of hidden expenses are also associated with outbreaks. Common expense factors to consider include loss of data, loss of productivity, damaged reputation, and loss of clientele.

Proactively planning against virus outbreaks, educating employees, maintaining a solid plan, up-training, and proactive efforts over time is how an organization needs to behave to avoid malware outbreaks.

Risk Analysis

Understanding what puts a computer at risk for a malware attack is an important step in formulating preventative measures. For example, a large company with employees that work at both home and office may have unique risks to their working environment. If employees use their own computers at home they may not have antivirus software installed or updated, helping spread viruses between home and work computers.

Assessment of security risks is a detailed and considerable task for large corporate environments. With all the new technologies, including local area networks (LANs), wide area networks (WANs), Internet connectivity, portable computing solutions, wireless communications, and more, new and unique risks abound.

Any time new media are brought into a computing environment there is a risk of compatibility issues, viruses, worms, Trojans, or other malware infections. It can be as simple as surfing the Internet and clicking on a malformed link while reading e-mail or accessing an infected disk from home.

Risk Factors

Various configurations, software settings, selected software, policies and procedures, and other security variables greatly affect the risks of acquiring a virus on an individual PC. Proper planning, well-thought-out policies, strong leadership in management, and maintenance plans considerably lower the risk of a malware infection.

Floppy disks

Floppy disks may carry boot sector viruses and malware within infected software on the disk. Floppy disks continue to be a source of infection for many users, especially home users. Even if a disk does not boot a system, it may still carry and infect a system with a boot sector infecting virus. Discouraging the use of floppy disks on a system is a good idea. Most media can easily be transferred through an Internet or intranet connection, avoiding the risk of infecting a computer with a boot sector virus. However, transferred files may still contain viruses and need to be managed appropriately.

Large corporations should carefully consider the risks and benefits associated with floppy disk access on a network. Removing floppy drives from desktop computers, changing the boot order, and disabling floppy boot capabilities are all great methods for removing the threat of a boot sector infection on a computer. If such policies and techniques are in place, with Internet connectivity enabled, employees may transfer files through a network instead of by floppy disk. Antivirus measures on the network may then work to protect the employee at home and the corporation.

No backups

Just about every computer user has lost something important on a computer at one time or another. Backing up data is very important, especially essential documents. Virus may inadvertently cause a system to crash, which may damage the contents of a hard drive. Other viruses, such as the CIH family, directly attack the PC, attempting to delete files from the hard drive. If no backup is in place, the user will likely lose important files, settings, and other configurations.

Even after a computer is infected, it's a good idea to back up files. Removing viruses from some files may corrupt them. Other viruses, such as ones that randomly overwrite files on a drive, may effectively erase a large number of files before they are detected and removed from a system. If a backup of important files is available, alternative removal and rescue strategies may be exercised to save the data. See the section on backup later in this chapter for more details on backing up files.

Black market software

Black market software is fairly common worldwide. New technologies, such as CD Read/Write drives, make it possible for people to create authentic-looking black market software. Others, such as the Internet, make it possible for individuals to illegally post copyrighted software, making it available for immediate download by Internet users.

Cases such as the infamous Chernobyl outbreak of 1999 clearly illustrate the danger of using black market software. As many as 600,000 users reportedly suffered from a Chernobyl virus infection, which erased files on the hard drive and attempted to corrupt the BIOS. Many of these users were located in Asia, where illegal copies of Windows and other popular software packages were illegally burned to CD ROM discs, accidentally including the Chernobyl virus in the burn.

No antivirus software installed

Many users simply don't have any antivirus software installed on their computers. Without any protection, users may not know that they are infected, often passing viruses along to others unknowingly. With free packages for both Macintosh and PC computers, there is no reason for any user to have no antivirus software installed. Even Macintosh users, which have relatively few software options compared to PC users, may still use Disinfectant, GateKeeper, Merryxmas Vaccine, and Microsoft Word macro protection tools to help prevent virus infections.

Old arguments about not having enough memory or hard drive space don't hold up either. With all the solutions in the freeware market for home users, such as F-Prot and InoculateIT PE, every basic need is adequately met. Even corporate users may obtain inexpensive solutions through various companies affordable by any business.

Outdated antivirus software

Perhaps one of the most alarming assumptions made by new computer users today is that their computer is protected by preloaded antivirus software. In most cases bundled software included on a new computer is burned to a disk months prior to the sale of a computer. Most new computer users use severely outdated software for months before updating an antivirus program.

Many users also make light of the need to update virus strings database files often. Updating only when one hears of a malicious outbreak In the Wild is like playing with fire—you might get burned! Progressive antivirus programs include automated features to update behind the scenes, without the need for user assistance after initial setup.

Others, such as large corporations with understaffed computing departments, simply don't take the time to update antivirus software. Updating antivirus software gets shuffled to the bottom of the tasks list on a regular basis. Taking such basic protection measures for granted is a good way to develop reactionary management strategies—always putting out fires instead of avoiding them in the first place. In the end it's the business that gets burned, especially employees. With advanced, and often automated, technical solutions for today's corporate network, there's no reason why all businesses can't be more proactive and easily protected against malware.

Installation not verified

Many users install software and assume it works as designed. Unlike a graphics program, where the user can see immediate and discernible results, an antivirus program is less obvious. How does one know that it has accurately scanned and found all viruses on a system? Perhaps it only looks like it's working but isn't scanning at all? Maybe it's scanning for viruses, but only those known to be In the Wild six months ago?

One classic example of a bad installation involves a large corporation with too little time. Reactively managing computer issues, staffing, and policies, employees in the computing department struggled just to get day to day tasks done on time. One of the first things to be dropped was proper desktop support and time spent verifying operations. In one situation an automated scan was set up on a desktop machine to log results only (no action taken if a virus is found), with a bad reference for the log file. The result was an antivirus program that scanned for viruses, did nothing, and was unable to log scan results. A few simple verification steps easily avoid such embarrassing and risky computing environments.

Fortunately there is a safe verification file, the EICAR test, that may be used to help verify antivirus software recently installed on a system. Simply use the newly installed antivirus software to scan an EICAR test file. If the EICAR test file is detected, the software is verified as installed and working good enough to detect the EICAR test. If not, consider reinstalling or reconfiguring the software before running a second EICAR test file. See Section 6 for detailed information on the EICAR test file and how to use it on your computer.

Incomplete removal of malware

Copies of malware are sometimes missed during detection and removal of malware on an infected system. A copy of Happy99.exe (SKA) may still reside in an e-mail letter, a Trojan may still be on a floppy disk, or an infected Word document may be lurking inside a compressed backup file. It's absolutely essential that users scan all media after removing malware from a system to avoid reinfecting the system. Using antivirus software to scan all files, in addition to manually going through suspect files, may help to detect and remove malware from other media.

Another consideration is the complete removal of all payloads and changes made to a system. Ethan, a Microsoft Word macro virus, is a good example of a virus with a visual payload that remains after the virus is removed from a system. Many users may think they are still infected with a virus because they see `Ethan Frome` as the suggested file name during a `Save As...` procedure, a visual payload of the Ethan virus. Simply updating infected documents with the correct properties avoids such confusion and misleading concerns about reinfection of a system.

Unprotected system

Leaving a system open and unprotected leaves not only the system at risk of infection but also the network if one is connected to the computer. For example, an employee in a large corporation decides to take a 15-minute break. During those 15 minutes a malicious user could easily access the system to obtain sensitive information such as logon rights, access to the local computer and network, and more. Much damage can be done in just 15 minutes!

As a matter of policy, all corporations should consider simple solutions such as asking employees to log off or lock out a computer when not in use. Simply pressing `CTRL-ALT-DELETE` enables an employee using Windows NT to lock out or log off of a system.

Administration should also have an Information Technology (IT) department in place that provides comprehensive network solutions for security and maintenance of a system. All too often management underbudgets such an operation, seriously impacting the performance and capabilities of the IT department.

Screen saver password

Screen saver password protection is an easy way to help protect a system while not in use. Simply right-click on the desktop of a Windows 95/98/NT/2000 machine and select Properties to access the Windows Display control panel. Click on the Screen Saver tab and click on the checkbox for Password protected. Click on the Change... button next to the Password protected checkbox to update the password as desired. Then set the screen saver wait time to the desired time period, such as 5 minutes. After the screen saver starts on a system, a password is required before access to the system may be obtained.

Microsoft Word and Excel protection

Current versions of Microsoft Word and Excel include protection options against macro viruses. Although Microsoft Office protection options are not failproof, they provide reasonable protection for the average user. Be aware that holes in Office security, such as printing from a disk, may bypass Microsoft Word macro protection, putting a computer at risk for a macro virus infection.

To enable macro virus protection, select Options from the Tools menu to access the options available for Microsoft Word. Click on the General tab and place a check next to Macro virus protection. Once this feature is enabled, the user is presented with a dialog box upon opening a Microsoft Word document containing a macro. Figure 5.1 is a screen shot from a typical macro protection dialog box.

The user may disable the macro, safely viewing the document without macro functionality. The other two options are to open the file with macros enabled or not to open the file at all. Because most users don't need to use macros to review or compose a Microsoft Word document, the disable option is a good choice for the average user. To learn more about the macro protection feature click on the `Tell Me More` button in Word or locate it within Microsoft Word help.

Office 2000 has enhanced macro virus protection built in for Microsoft Word, Excel, PowerPoint, and Outlook. Users may select `Security` from the `Tools` menu of any one of these programs to set the security to low, medium, or high. Figure 5.2 shows a screen shot of a standard Office 2000 security dialog box, including the antivirus software status on the computer.

Low settings are not recommended for individuals concerned about macro viruses. Medium security provides users with an option to disable or enable macros as they are encountered in documents being opened— much like older versions of macro protection. High security includes trusted resources, which can be managed by a network administrator remotely.

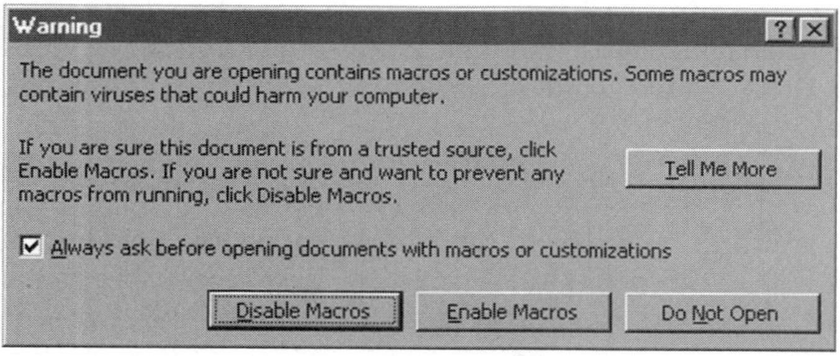

Figure 5.1   Microsoft Word macro protection.

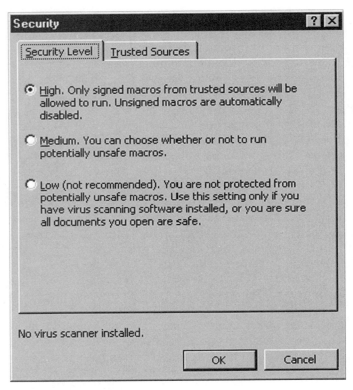

Figure 5.2 Office 2000 security.

Trusted resources are digitally signed and accepted sources; the security software attempts to verify the authenticity of the sender. If a network manager identifies a source that is considered high risk, he or she may remove the source from the trusted resources list. This effectively blocks content on computers with Office 2000 configured with high security.

Adding passwords to Microsoft Word documents helps to protect against unauthorized access. If a file is locked, set to read only, or protected by a password, it lowers the risk of infection. To add a password to a Microsoft Word document simply select Save As...

from the `File` menu and click on the `Options` button. Passwords may be entered to protect the document from being opened as well as against modifications after being opened. A checkbox item for making a document read-only is also available.

See the Tips and Techniques area, later in this section, to learn how to protect `normal.dot`.

Microsoft Outlook

Microsoft Outlook and Microsoft Outlook Express programs are popular e-mail, usenet, and business utility tools. They are used by a large number of PC users worldwide. They are also the targets of many e-mail exploits, including BubbleBoy and Kak.Worm malware. Turning off auto-preview options is an easy way to lower risks associated with such malware.

Various versions of Outlook and other programs have different methods for disabling automated features such as auto-preview. To disable such a feature, the rule of thumb is to access the options or preferences of a program and search for automated functions that can be disabled. For example, in Outlook Express 4.X users simply select `Layout` from the `View` menu to remove the checkmark from the `Use preview pane` option. In Outlook, remove the check from `Preview Pane` in the `View` menu to disable auto-preview.

Once auto-preview is disabled, Outlook users simply double-click on messages to view them, opening a separate e-mail window. The e-mail window has a header window that displays the transfer information and the subject of the e-mail. The lower frame in the e-mail window contains the content of the e-mail, as shown in Figure 5.3.

When e-mail programs require that users double-click on a message to view the contents, they are not running special scripts or commands that may be easily exploited. One may think of opening e-mail in this manner as simply reading text on the screen—there's

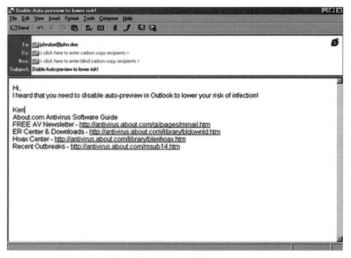

Figure 5.3 Auto-preview disabled in Outlook.

nothing special about the functionality or scripts running in the background that might put your computer at risk.

E-mail attachments

E-mail is one of the easiest and most common methods for malware to enter a system or network. As a general policy, accepting attachments from others is to be discouraged. In the past, attachments of type .doc or .exe were flagged as potentially dangerous, whereas attachments of type .jpg and .gif were considered safe. New exploits have put all file types and attachments under greater scrutiny, forcing users to be extremely careful about accepting any attachment from another user—even an individual known to the recipient.

Sending files in formats such as Rich Text Files (.rtf) or text (.txt) is considered less risky than .doc and .exe attachments. If a text file is opened within NotePad it does not contain a macro or possible macro virus—it's simply text, nothing else. RTFs are popular with some users because they maintain formatting not supported by plain text files. RTF files may be safely opened and viewed in WordPad, with reasonable formatting supported.

Because malware like Kak.Worm exploits both Outlook and Internet Explorer, it's important to update Internet Explorer with security patches and upgrades as they become available on the Microsoft Internet site.

Browser security

Internet Explorer and Netscape Navigator are two popular Internet browsers used by users all around the world to access files and information on the Internet. Internet Explorer appears to be a common target for security exploits. Another reason why it is more commonly exploited is how it is integrated with other Microsoft products.

As the complexity and sheer amount of code increases for integrated and enhanced Microsoft solutions, Microsoft products naturally develop new bugs and open new security holes for hackers to exploit. Netscape, and all other software for that matter, faces a similar scenario. What makes Internet Explorer different is that it is more closely integrated with the Windows operating system and common office applications, including Microsoft Word, Excel, Powerpoint, and Access.

Some users switch to other browsers, such as Netscape, to avoid attacks and problems associated with Internet Explorer. Regardless of what browser one uses, it's important to obtain updates and patches on a regular basis. Check the sponsoring Internet site often for updates, stay informed with newsletters and reputable sites on the Internet, and take the time to stay up on the basics of the antivirus industry.

Making use of available security options within a browser may also help lower the risk of infection. In

Internet Explorer 4.X, select `Internet Options...` from the `View` menu and click on the `Security` tab to access security options. Click on the level of security desired for each zone and apply the changes. Some users avoid the high setting, since it may interrupt normal browsing experiences on the Internet. See the `Content` tab and other tabs for additional security options, such as certificates, content advisor, and Java.

Netscape 4.X users may change security settings by selecting `Preferences...` from the `Edit` menu. Click on the `Advanced` preference option to enable or disable features such as Java and JavaScript support.

Downloading software

With millions of pages available on the Internet, it's getting to be more and more difficult for users to discern reputable sites from the disreputable. Before the use of HyperText Transfer Protocol (HTTP) became the Internet standard, the number of well-known reputable sites could be printed on a few pages. Today is a much different story, with millions of Internet users, many of which even have their own Web pages.

Downloading files from disreputable sites greatly increases the risk of infection on a computer. Download sites to avoid include obscure, personal, and unprofessional sites. Reputable sites, such as Microsoft, CNET, and About.com, all scan available files and downloads for viruses before making such files available to users for downloading. After all, they don't want a virus any more than the customer does.

Disreputable sites may be run by an individual that doesn't even have antivirus software. Additionally, reputable sites have something at stake, their name. It's important to every business to maintain a positive image. A single media report about a virus outbreak on a site can irreparably harm a company long term. Disreputable sites have little concern or less at stake regarding such issues. Downloading from reputable sites is always recommended when available.

After downloading files, be sure to scan them for viruses before extracting the compressed file. After extraction, scan the files again, just to make sure. Some antivirus programs do a great job of scanning extracted files but don't perform as well with certain types of compressed files.

Zip file protection

Zip files are compressed files, made smaller for backup purposes, saving space on a drive, securing an archive, or transferring files quickly through an intranet or the Internet. Adding a password to an archive while it's being saved will make it more difficult for users to accidentally open, infect, or modify an archive. If using a program like WinZip, simply click on the Password... button when creating a Zip archive to add a password to the compressed file.

View options

For example, one method for spreading viruses is to send users an attachment such as fun.jpg.exe, where a large number of characters (mostly spaces) for a Windows file name is utilized. Many users believe the file to be a JPG image file, not seeing the .exe under icon view or with preferences not showing extensions of files. Changing the view of a computer to show the extension of a file helps users to identify the true function of a file in question.

Network security and config-uration

Corporations often neglect network antivirus technology options such as firewalls, proxy servers, and e-mail scanners. Such options are very cost effective when compared to the cost of a virus outbreak. Ironically, such systems are sometimes in place for content security on the Internet but not for antivirus measures. The IT department ideally needs to be the backbone of all antivirus measures, implementing network options prior to desktop solutions. Good network plans are closely tied to policy and procedure and training of employees.

Assessing the need of desktop users is another important consideration for network configurations. For example, a large organization may have a few developers authoring files in Microsoft Word and a large number of users that merely need to read the Microsoft Word files. In such a scenario a company may install Microsoft Word on all local machines, enable users to use Word through a server, or use a Word viewer or plug-in application for read-only users.

Local installations are more difficult and time consuming than a server solution. On the other side of the coin, server solutions are bandwidth-intensive. Ideally the company would enable developers to use Word through a server and all other users to use a viewer or plug-in utility to view Microsoft Word documents. If configured correctly, only the developers pose a risk of infection to macro viruses, which may be scanned by network solutions and a local on-access scanner.

Carefully controlling user rights and profiles on a network is another important consideration for network system operators. In the example above the developers could easily be configured on a network through a user profile with networking solutions such as Windows NT. Employing options such as account lockouts, password control, full path executable validation (block external launches), and group rights helps administrators to easily control large groups of individual accounts from a single console and group profile.

Network solutions also give employees the freedom to move from computer to computer, maintaining group rights and configurations as they move. Administrators may also easily automate multiple features, including antivirus updates. Even if an infection occurs on a client PC, network rights and access assigned to each user lower the risk of infection to networked PCs.

Lack of policy and procedure

Failure to have policy and procedure in place in a corporate environment is asking for trouble. Good policy and procedure is a practical, legitimate, easy-to-follow plan for which all employees are accountable. Poor policies, or implementation, are often rejected by employees, rendering them useless. Carefully planning out policies and procedures based upon unique needs and proactive thinking is just as important as working to have all employees support new policies and procedures. See the section on policies and procedures later in this chapter for details on how to create and implement solid antivirus policies and procedures.

Lack of education

All too often employees don't know what a virus is, how to detect it, or what to do if they suspect an infection. The knowledge gap between network or computer administrators and employees is large in many corporations. Involving training departments in all elements of the business greatly assists efforts in effectively implementing and maintaining antivirus efforts in a business.

No alert system

Establishing and maintaining an effective communications plan is a major challenge for growing businesses. Because virus technology changes often, every business should consider developing and implementing a virus alert system. Working closely with employees in developing such a tool will make such an initiative be successful, valued, and utilized.

Antivirus Software Configuration

Improperly configured antivirus programs compromise the security of a system. Reviewing configurations, and then verifying correct operation, are the two critical aspects of successfully installing antivirus software. Corporate managers need to make sure that IT departments are well supported with both finances and staff.

Scanning options

Antivirus programs offer a wide variety of scanning options. It's very important for a user to make sure that all compatible scanning options are enabled on a system for the maximum protection. It's also important to understand the differences between various scanning options. For example, some on-access scanners are not as robust as on-demand scanners but do offer reasonable on-access protection.

Scan during startup. Scanning a computer for viruses, before it even boots up completely, is a great idea. Solutions such as the ChipAway Virus Protection program use hardware added on to the motherboard to scan for viruses prior to launching Windows on a PC computer. Most commercial antivirus programs also offer users an option to run a scan upon startup. Two major disadvantages to running a scan during startup are the wait time and lack of on-access protection after startup. Because of performance issues, most scanners only scan by default program files or selected directories, such as the Windows System folder.

On-access scanning. On-access scanners help to protect users while they work. To avoid performance issues, many antivirus on-access scanners are set to scan program files only as they are accessed rather than scanning all files on a computer. Because the default setting of on-access scanners is rarely set to scan all files and because sometimes they are not as robust as on-demand scanners, they do not always offer the best protection possible. Carefully configuring scanning options and combining on-access scanning with other types of scans is highly recommended.

On-demand scanning. On-demand scanning is a robust way for users to manually scan a system for viruses. Manually running a scan on a regular basis is strongly recommended, especially when a new file, disk, or other medium is brought into a system. Making use of both on-access and on-demand scanners on a system is an excellent way to avoid malware infections on a computer. For example, saving an e-mail attachment to the hard drive, performing an on-demand scan of the attachment, and then opening it with an on-access scanner running in the background provides a reasonable level of scanning security on a system.

Scan during shutdown. Scans during shutdown are sometimes better received than startup scans. Once a user has completed work on a computer and initiated a shutdown, antivirus software may then scan the system for viruses. Some programs even help against boot sector virus infections by prompting the user to remove any floppy disks left in a drive during shutdown. This effectively avoids a boot sector virus infection that could have occurred if the system was booted from an infected floppy disk.

Scheduling comprehensive scans. Scheduling comprehensive on-demand scans is an excellent way to help protect a system. Scheduling utilities contained with suite packages and some antivirus programs enable users to easily schedule the date, time, type of scan, and frequency of scanning.

One problem with scheduled scans in a corporate environment involves users that cancel scans initiated while the computer is in use. Use a scheduling utility to scan computers on lunch breaks or when a computer is normally not in use. If performance lags are experienced during scheduled scans, reschedule scans to take place when the computer is not in use.

Types of scans

On-demand and on-access scanners both offer a variety of scanning options. Changing scan options may affect the performance on a machine when the scan is executed. If a comprehensive scan takes up too much memory or results in a dramatic drop in system performance, consider using less comprehensive scan options on a regular basis, running more comprehensive scans on a less frequent or as-needed basis.

If scanning options discussed here are not in your version of software, consider upgrading your current package or exploring options available in other antivirus programs. The "Try before you buy" concept of trialware downloads on the Internet offers many users an option to use a commercial program before they buy it.

Scanning individual files and folders. Most programs enable users to scan individual files or folders on a drive. Some make it as easy as right-clicking on a file and selecting a virus scan option in the pop-up menu that appears. Others require that you double-click on a taskbar icon or run the on-demand program to identify and scan individual files or folders.

Program only scanning. A common default setting, especially for on-access scanners, is to scan only program files. When a program is opened or closed, it may be scanned for viruses. This type of scanning method is very efficient at the expense of scanning all files as they are accessed.

All files scanning. Scanning all files is a much more detailed and time-consuming scanning option. Most users will notice a drop in performance after selecting a "dumb" scan of all files. Scanning all files is recommended, on a regular basis, with an on-demand scanner. Since a scan of all files normally takes a while, initiate scans to occur while the computer is not in use, such as when leaving for a lunch break or just before leaving work for the evening.

Heuristic scanning. Although heuristic scanning is constantly being integrated into virus detection technology, specific heuristic engines are available on several commercial applications. Heuristic scan options may offer sensitivity settings for heuristic scans, where the user can enable strong or weak heuristic controls, as shown in Figure 5.4. If strong or high sensitivity controls are enabled, the user may experience a number of false alarms—suspected viruses that are not viral at all. Most users set heuristic scanning options to medium sensitivity or below to avoid constant false alarms.

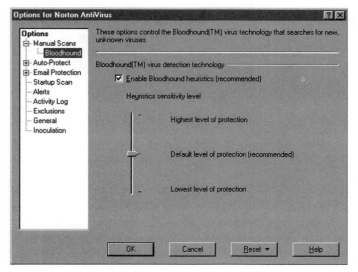

Figure 5.4 Heuristic options in Norton Antivirus 2000.

Internet scanning. Several antivirus programs now provide users with Web-based Internet filter and security options. As new technologies are exploited In the Wild, such options will become more important. A trend in the antivirus industry is to develop future software solutions that offer complete security protection rather than just focusing on security against computer viruses.

Action taken. A variety of actions are supported by various commercial antivirus programs: clean or repair infected file, rename infected file, quarantine file in question, deny access, record the event to a log file, e-mail administrator, and notify the user with an alert message or sound. Some programs also support an `Ask` feature, where the user is prompted for the appropriate action to take when a virus is found on a system.

Many users simply select `clean`, wanting to remove any viruses found on a system. Unfortunately, the removing of virus strings from an infected program or file during the cleaning process may corrupt a file or leave it in an unusable state. Saving a backup copy of an essential infected file prior to cleaning is a good idea. This way several different programs or rescue methods may be employed if an essential document is not easily cleaned by the first antivirus program that detected a virus in the file.

Selecting an option such as `rename` or `quarantine` may be a better option for a user that needs to rescue an important file infected with a virus. Placing an infected document into a quarantine directory assigned by antivirus software puts the infected file in a known quarantine location where files are treated with caution. It also removes the infected file from future scans. Some antivirus programs, such as PC-cillin, enable users to easily work with quarantined files to submit them to the company for analysis, attempt to clean a quarantined file, restore or add a file to the directory of quarantined files, or delete files in question, as shown in Figure 5.5.

Positive and negative results. Antivirus software may render false-positive, false-negative, and ghost-positive reports.

A false positive is more commonly referred to as a false alarm. Sometimes legitimate software is detected as a virus when, in fact, it is not infected with a virus. False positives sometimes are more common when high heuristic settings are used by antivirus software to detect and remove viruses from a system.

A false negative is when a virus program fails to detect a virus on a system. False negatives are more often an issue with new viruses or highly modified variants of an existing family In the Wild. See Section 6 for detailed tables of antivirus programs and their ability to detect and remove malware In the Wild.

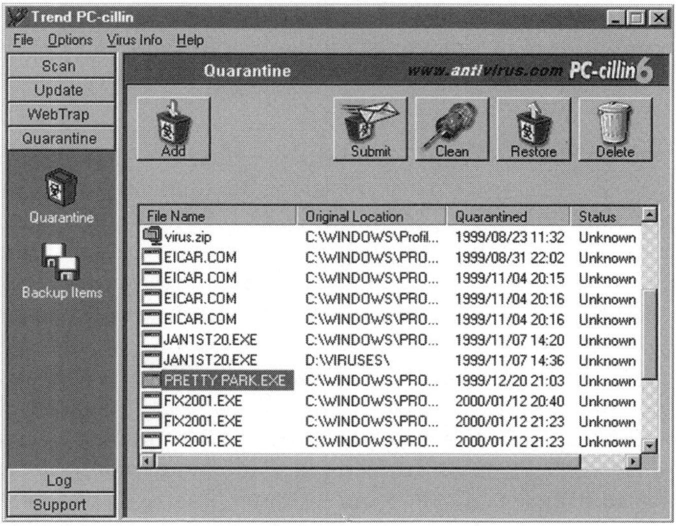

Figure 5.5 PC-cillin 6.X quarantine file options.

Ghost positives are the result of inactive, disabled, or remnants of a virus being identified as a virus threat on a system. Portions of virus code may be left behind during the removal process. If a different antivirus program is used to scan the system at a later date, a remnant of the disabled virus may be detected as an infection.

Ghost positives may also be the result of one antivirus scanner being confused by another recently run in memory. Always restart a system before using a second scanning program, especially when conflicting results are found. Another good idea is to defragment a disk using the "clean slack space" (if available); sometimes removing fragments causes ghost positives.

Hardware Configuration

Some hardware configurations and antivirus solutions may help to avoid virus infections. Since hardware is not easily updated, solutions are normally limited to protecting against older, well-known viruses In the Wild. Hardware antivirus protection offers a complement to robust antivirus software solutions and other preventative measures.

CMOS boot sequence

CMOS, complementary metal oxide semiconductor, is nonvolatile static RAM (SRAM) that stores configuration information for a computer system. Although it's possible for a virus to change CMOS settings, as seen with the EXE_Bug virus, there are no known viruses that are able to infect, hide, or replicate in CMOS. Infection and replication from the CMOS is highly improbable for a variety of highly technical reasons.

Using the CMOS to change the boot sequence helps to avoid boot sector infections. Many new computers are configured to boot from a floppy disk first, if available, before booting from the hard drive. If supported, simply press the appropriate function key during startup, as shown on the screen, to change the CMOS boot sequence to boot from the hard disk first.

Use this same basic process in the future if a need arises to boot from a floppy disk temporarily, changing the boot sequence back to booting from a floppy disk first.

Trend ChipAway Virus protection

The Trend ChipAway Virus (TCAV), developed by Trend Micro Systems, Inc., is a virus protection option that is sometimes misinterpreted by users as a virus. TCAV loads with read-only memory (ROM) basic in/out system (BIOS) when a computer is first booted up.

TCAV prevents boot sector viruses from infecting a system by running in memory before a computer is booted from a disk. TCAV uses rules-based Virus Trap Technology to detect known and unknown boot sector viruses by behavior rather than with virus string databases. Updates are not required for TCAV to be fully effective.

Network Protection

The availability and robust functionality of network protection tools on the market today provide IT managers with some outstanding security tools. Administrators need to carefully author strategic plans to consider the need and risk assessment for use of floppy disks, Internet access, encryption, internal communication, and other considerations. Disabling all unnecessary hardware and software does lower the risk of a malware infection.

Firewalls and proxy servers

Firewalls and proxy servers enable network administrators to restrict access to networks, defining and configuring security policies to help protect against attacks from both inside and outside of a company.

Firewalls and proxy servers enable administrators to set alarms, log events, report violations of security policies, and easily update security policies from a centralized station.

One important firewall and proxy server consideration for antivirus protection is to protect and validate all opened ports. Remote access tools (RAT) malware, such as Back Orifice, opens a back door to a network by opening a port for a hacker to exploit with a remote access tool. As long as the port remains open, a hacker has access to one or more systems on the network. Monitoring all unused ports not already dedicated to a specific network function helps protect against network attacks.

Another network consideration involves shared resources. Internet users may exploit shared resources on a network, as seen with the 911 worm. Disable NetBIOS over TCP/IP to prevent an exploitation of shared resources on a network. To check the settings for NetBIOS, open the `Network` control panel in Windows 95/98/NT, select `TCP/IP`, and click on the `Properties` button. Click on the `NetBIOS` tab and remove the checkmark from the `I want to enable NetBIOS over TCP/IP` checkbox if selected. Another method for identifying the setup is to type `NETSTAT -A` in the DOS prompt to see if ports 137, 138, and 139 appear.

Network antivirus

Network antivirus software solutions offer a variety of protection options that need to be exploited by administrators to scan local drives, network drives, and e-mail. Considering each medium, and implementing appropriate antivirus measures, is an important part of a successful corporate plan.

One unique way to protect a network is to use a Linux server with antivirus software to scan all network media for viruses. Linux is not easily infected with a virus and is a free, open-source stable operating system that can be very easily configured and run on a low-cost server by an experienced administrator.

Another good idea for network protection is to run an integrity check program to detect unauthorized changes made to applications on servers. Detected changes can be inspected to rule out or remove malware infections.

Centralized administration

Using centralized antivirus software tools, remote access tools such as PC Anywhere, and strategies like imaging drives and remotely installing antivirus solutions to a workstation enable network managers to quickly and effectively manage networks of any size. For companies with more than just a handful of computers that are networked, centralized administration should be a serious consideration for as many network solutions as possible, especially antivirus.

Common network administration options include alerts, scanning enforcement, network and local configurations, scheduling, updates and upgrades, remote cleanup and repair, logging and reporting events, analysis of network events, status, and history.

Emergency Software Everyone Should Have

Be prepared! Having proper emergency, boot, and antivirus disks on hand enables a user to remove viruses from a system and initiate repairs quickly. When creating such disks, clearly label them and lock them by moving the plastic tab up (see a hole through the disk casing). Locking a disk prevents software changes, blocking all malware attempts to infect a disk.

Emergency disk

Windows NT users may create an "emergency repair disk" during installation of the operating system or when running RDISK on the computer. An emergency disk does not boot (start up) a computer. An emergency disk contains backup registry files that may be used by Windows NT during a rescue operation. Creating an emergency disk after installing a system or major update is a good idea. If major errors are found on the computer, the emergency disk may be used in the troubleshooting process to repair the computer.

Boot disk

A boot disk is a disk that is capable of starting up a computer. DOS boot disks contain special files, two of which are hidden on the disk, that are required to start up a computer.

Boot disks are an essential tool to have on hand at all times. Some viruses are not easily removed from a system, requiring a boot disk to gain exclusive control over a system. Once exclusive control is gained, antivirus software may be run to remove a virus from an infected system.

To gain exclusive control users should power down and literally turn off the power to a computer for about 30 seconds to clear all instructions running in memory. Insert a locked boot disk into the computer and turn it back on, booting from the floppy disk. Then run antivirus software from a different floppy or CD—not from a potentially infected hard drive.

When starting up a computer the CMOS/BIOS settings may need to be changed to enable the computer to start up from the floppy disk in drive A. Press the appropriate key shown on the screen, such as F2 or Delete, to enter CMOS/BIOS startup options if a system does not boot from the floppy disk as desired.

Many users also put extra files on a boot disk to increase functionality and options during an emergency situation. Table 5.1 identifies common programs that some users place on a boot disk, space permitting.

See Section 6 for instructions on how to create a boot disk for PC and Macintosh operating systems.

TABLE 5.1   **Files to consider using on a boot disk**

Boot Disk Files	Description
autoexec.bat	A foundational file used during startup of a computer.
CD ROM driver	Copy over CD ROM driver if available.
chkdsk.exe	Checks disk for errors, makes minor repairs, and displays information about the disk. Updated DOS, 6.0 or later, users may use Scandisk instead.
config.sys	A foundational file used during startup of a computer.
fdisk.exe	Remove master boot record viruses from the hard drive with FDISK /MBR, or repartition drives. Use this program with extreme caution!
format.com	Formats disks as desired.
mem.exe	MEM verifies normal memory setup on a computer when compared against known "normal" memory settings. Abnormal readings may indicate an infection.
unformat.exe	DOS 5.0 or later may use UNFORMAT /L /PARTN to verify normal configurations for partitions on a drive.
scandisk.exe	Scans and corrects disks for basic errors.
scandisk.ini	Initializes the scandisk.exe program. Copy over with Scandisk.
sys.com	Overwrites DOS partition of an infected hard drive with SYS C: command.

Antivirus software on disk or CD

Having antivirus software on a disk or CD prior to a virus infection is an ideal plan. If a virus infection is detected or suspected, antivirus software may be run from the disk or CD after booting from a clean floppy disk to remove a virus. This method gives the user exclusive control over a system, enabling him or her to easily remove most malware from a system.

If antivirus software is located on a floppy disk, simply remove the boot disk and insert the antivirus disk.

Then use DOS commands like `DIR` to see the contents of the disk. Type in the name of a program, of `.exe` or `.com` extension, to run antivirus software located on the floppy disk. For example, if a file called `f-prot.exe` was listed on the disk the user would type `f-prot` to run the program.

If antivirus software is located on a CD ROM disc, support files to be able to access the CD ROM drive need to be included on the floppy disk. If so, a user simply enters a DOS command like `D:` to access the contents of the CD ROM (D drive in this example). After accessing the drive, commands like `DIR` are used to locate files and folders on the CD ROM. Once the program is located, it is entered and run in DOS. Some antivirus programs provide simple instructions to follow to easily run antivirus from a CD ROM disc when working in a DOS environment.

See Section 6 for instructions on how to place a copy of F-Prot antivirus on disk for emergency situations. See Appendix C for a list of common DOS commands and how to use them.

Policies and Procedures

Clearly defined and implemented policies and procedures are the most effective proactive management tool currently available.

Essential elements of policies and procedures

Using the KISS principle, Keeping It Simple for Success, is a good guideline for any new policy or procedure. Effective policies and procedures have to be simple and practical enough that people will follow them. For example, if a user needs to have a disk scanned by another individual, who isn't always available, he or she may end up just using the disk without waiting. Pages and pages of policy aren't well received by employees either. A few elements to consider when drafting new antivirus policies and procedures and implementation plans are outlined below:

- Clearly define terminology, such as malware and trusted/untrusted sites.

- Proactive measures for both employees and management to take, such as enabling Microsoft Word macro virus protection and scanning disks and attachments before use.

- Risk assessment considerations, including things such as traveling floppy disks and e-mail.

- Computer access considerations, such as not allowing certain individuals to use a computer or have certain access rights on the network.

- Current antivirus solutions and maintenance plans, including updates and upgrades to antivirus software.

Network security plan

Network security covers everything from proper physical security to user identification security. Carefully analyzing and considering all security needs is an important proactive step. Businesses may benefit from paying a third-party source to assess their needs, or researching and seeing what other businesses do to secure their systems.

Consider the following for physical security of network equipment:

- Restrict access to servers, placing them in a locked room of sufficient size, with sufficient air conditioning and power.

- Limit the number of individuals with access to server equipment.

- Use uninterruptable power supplies for all servers and related equipment.

■ Secure all equipment by attaching it to shelving, cables, or furniture, in case of earthquake or theft attempts.

■ Label equipment and create a map of equipment location and functionality.

Consider the following for user identification security:

■ Provide each user with a unique logon.

■ Require that passwords have a minimum length, mixed alphanumeric characters, mixed case, changed on a regular basis.

■ Limit the number of users with administrative rights on the network.

■ Disable or delete user identifications immediately upon an individual leaving the company.

In addition to the basic infrastructure of security explained above, corporations will want to have practical use policies to protect against malware attacks. Examples include only allowing employees to use authorized software on a computer and reporting all malware incidents to the IT department. Address the following guidelines when developing a practical plan:

■ Keep It Simple for Success—Antivirus solutions on the desktop should basically be transparent, not requiring much of the desktop user, if anything at all. Relying on staff to run daily antivirus scans is a bad idea, since not every staff member will follow the rules.

■ Accountability—Make sure that users do not have the ability, or do not change the settings on a computer, disabling or hampering the ability for chosen antivirus software to run as desired. Record a log file and review it on a regular basis to monitor activity on workstations.

▪ Remote Updates—Run all software updates and upgrades to a workstation from a remote location, requiring no work or knowledge on the part of the employee using the workstation being updated.

▪ Compatibility—Select an antivirus solution that best meets the needs of workstations in an organization.

Carefully identify the procedures for discipline if a policy is violated, and implement a solid education plan to empower employees to value and make good use of a new policy or procedure. A final consideration is the development of an antivirus support team or assigned individuals ready in the IT department to deal with virus incidences as they occur. When developing such a group, consider the following:

▪ Select a small group of capable members from across the organization, with a majority of the group being composed of individuals from the IT department. This way all issues, from training to technical issues, can be better addressed by the entire organization.

▪ Assign individuals to be points of contact for various portions of the organization.

▪ Create a mailing list and contact cards for each member to give to individuals in the organization on an as-needed basis.

▪ Establish a communication process to inform all members of virus incidents and immediate needs.

▪ Establish efficient antivirus prevention, containment, recovery, and repair strategies. For example, imaging common desktop setups to quickly repair damaged computers remotely through a network.

▪ Have high expectations for the team and communicate possible requirements such as weekend work and crisis intervention.

Acceptable use policy

Implementing an acceptable use policy or contract provides employers with an opportunity to clearly explain to employees the acceptable use guidelines for a computing system. If employees violate the agreement, employers have a legal document on which to rely, holding the employee accountable for his or her actions.

If an acceptable use policy is not already in place in an organization, management may benefit from involving all levels of employees in the constructive development of a new acceptable use policy. Employees will oftentimes have great ideas or perspectives that management may not have considered.

Focus groups are a great way to involve a wide range of employees in constructing new policy or procedure without having to involve every single employee in an organization. Focus groups need to have a clear goal and structure and involve a wide range of employees within an organization. Clearly stating the purpose of a focus group, providing participants with support media, and encouraging brainstorming of ideas are all important elements of a successful focus session.

The leader of a focus group needs to carefully summarize and honor all input, asking for clarification as required and feedback from individuals who have not participated until a wide variety of information has been identified and discussed by the group. Some brainstorming sessions do benefit from literally writing all ideas on a board before wading through them as a group. Others benefit from a leader that carefully listens to input and summarizes major ideas on a board as they are discussed.

Following up with the same focus group after management has considered the input and drafted a plan helps to refine and polish a policy or procedure before it is implemented by management. If a policy or procedure is rejected by the focus group, additional sessions may be necessary to better understand and address the issues at hand. If a policy or procedure merely needs minor revisions, management can be reasonably secure that other employees in the company will accept the new policy or procedure.

Ideally, an acceptable use contract or new policy and procedure will be reviewed by a company representative with employees prior to signing. Simply giving the paperwork to an employee to sign and return does not adequately address or place enough importance upon the acceptable use contract to ensure success. Some employees asked to simply sign and return a contract may not fully understand the reasoning and motives behind various directives, passively ignoring or violating the policy at a later date.

Content of an overall policy and procedure plan should answer the following:

- Who the policy affects and why it is needed.

- The authority figure in charge of the policy.

- Legal information as required to protect the company and employee.

- Process for implementing and maintaining the policy.

- Information to be protected and how the protection shall be accomplished.

- Software allowed on employee computers.

- Activities allowed and not allowed, such as downloading software from the Internet.

- Expectations and procedures for reporting security violations.

- Consequences for when an employee violates the policy.

- Who enforces the policy and how enforcement is accomplished.

- Explanations of the policy, with examples when possible.

■ Use concise, appropriate, positive language in the policy whenever possible.

After answering questions like those listed previously, carefully discern a strategic plan to identify the content of user policies, system policies, and detailed procedures. Keep user policies, such as an acceptable use policy, clear and concise for success. A sample acceptable use policy for corporations is given below:

Acceptable Use Policy

Company Name & Logo, John Doe, 111-555-5555, john-doe@example.com.

Company Name encourages the sharing of information and use of computers within the organization. There is an obligation on the part of those using business facilities and services to respect the security and rights of others and the business as a whole.

Appropriate Use Guidelines

Employees and supported vendors may use *Company Name* computer and network services under the following conditions:

■ All activity must be lawful and proper, in accordance with *Company Name* business initiatives and purpose. Obscene, harassing, or threatening communication is prohibited.

■ Transmission, resale, or communication of proprietary, confidential company information outside of business staff is prohibited.

■ Any technical disruption or unauthorized access to computers or the network is prohibited.

■ Intentionally accessing sensitive information, such as logon rights or password access, is prohibited.

■ The following activities are prohibited: sending out 25 or more unsolicited e-mails, use of chat software or Internet chat rooms, accessing newsgroups, downloading software, accessing adult-oriented sites or information, or engaging in personal/non-business or personal-profit-related activities.

Company Name determines who is in violation of this policy, at the sole discretion of the currently appointed security manager. Violations of this policy may result in termination without notice.

_____

Employee Signature   Date

_____

Security Manager   Date

School guidelines

Schools will want to adopt an acceptable use policy that is similar to the corporate example provided in the previous section. When developing appropriate use guidelines and an antivirus plan for a school district, consider the following unique elements:

- Include educational information in a school-related policy to help students, parents, teachers, and administrators understand the document. Be specific when clarifying guidelines.

- Encourage students to bring disks to and from home. This promotes the learning environment in the home and better enables students to complete projects that make use of computers. Bolting down a lab of computers for fear of viruses is the wrong approach to educating our children. Providing them with a structured environment that is reasonable and fair, with guidelines for appropriate use and associated consequences, empowers students for success.

- Dedicate one or more computers for virus scanning if there is a limited budget for antivirus scanning on all machines. Using a nonnetworked machine for scanning viruses is also a good idea because it lowers the risk of infecting the entire network if a virus is on media being scanned.

▪ Don't be afraid to use free antivirus scanners until you can acquire long-term commercial antivirus solutions. Some of the best solutions are often free, especially when they target a specific virus recently found In the Wild. Just make sure that the antivirus solution chosen adequately protects computers against infection. Free software, such as Merryxmas Vaccine for HyperCard on the Macintosh, are an excellent supplement to a commercial antivirus program.

▪ Provide students with free antivirus solutions, a computing newsletter, tips and tricks. Educating the entire community better justifies expenditures for technology in a school district while lowering the overall risk of infection for computers within the community.

▪ Try creative solutions such as inviting parents to a free evening class to teach them the basics of computers and antivirus. Another idea is to have a computer club that helps with antivirus efforts in the school system. Providing reports for a school newspaper on the number of infections and tips and tricks on how to avoid them, along with malware description of the day, will help educate students and staff while promoting a virus-free environment in the school.

Parent-child contract

Parents may benefit from having a parent-child contract in place prior to a child using a computer in the home. Developing the contract with a child helps the child to better receive and appreciate a contract—rather than simply making a child sign a contract that may be meaningless or seemingly unfair to them.

Parents may want to start the contract process by asking their child to write down what the rules of the contract should be. Parents can do the same and then compare notes with the child, discussing the rules as the contract is drafted. This gives parents an opportunity to identify what is required, what is desired, and what their child thinks is fair and appropriate. Be flexible with ideas from the child, honoring their input in the contract as long as it does not directly conflict with essential elements identified by the parent. Make sure that the "why" behind each rule is considered and discussed for every rule in the contract. Try to keep the rules to a minimum, making a contract easy to follow and understand, especially for younger children.

After the rules are drafted, use the same procedure to identify appropriate consequences if rules are broken. Ask the child to formulate consequences that logically match the violation of various rules in the contract. For example, if a child downloads and runs a new game found on the Internet, without parent permission, the consequence might be that the child loses the ability to use the Internet, or the computer, for a certain amount of time. After comparing notes between the parent and child, draft the consequences into the contract. Make sure all possibilities, with some room for the parent to discern appropriate consequences, are included in the contract. Adding a line such as, "*Parent Name* reserves the right to change or void this contract at any time" helps a child to understand that the parent is still in charge (and may overrule), even though there is a contract in place. Follow up with a discussion regarding the child following the spirit of the contract, avoid arguments over legalistic interpretations.

Add a signature block for the parent and the child and give a copy to the child when done signing. You might even want to give them the pen used in the signing to humor them, as if they just signed a major contract or bought a house. In all seriousness, do make sure the contract is posted in a visible location, such as near the computer or on the refrigerator.

Closely monitor and help the child to be successful with the new contract, installing filtering, security, or antivirus software as required. Don't unreasonably expect a child to simply follow the rules, even when a parent is around. Monitor and hold the child accountable until he or she gains the trust and right to have more independence. Placing the computer in an area of the home that is more open, rather than secluded or cut off, will also help to hold computer users accountable.

Avoid providing children with any incentives for following the contract, other than simply using the computer—the reward should only be the right to use the computer.

A sample parent-child contract is given below as a guideline in constructing your own parent-child contract. Avoid big or confusing words for contracts developed with younger children. Covering all of your "legal" grounds with a child is not the point—a clear understanding of what is expected, and fair, is what must be communicated between the parent and child. If there are concerns about elements such as Internet access, research it with other parents and consultants before allowing the child to use the tool. Another option is to use the tool in question, with the child, to better understand it as a parent and model for the child.

Computer Contract

This document shall govern the computer use in the home for *Child Name*, until further notice. *Parent Name* reserves the right to change or void this contract at any time.

Access is allowed for:

1. E-mail
2. Internet Web pages
3. Downloading of software or attachments

Access is NOT allowed for:

1. Chat rooms or chat software

2. Newsgroups, discussion boards, or bulletin boards

3. Creating or posting Web pages

4. Anything else not specifically identified in the allowed section. Get permission from *Parent Name* first.

Appropriate use guidelines

Use of the computer should always be done with a good heart and thankfulness for the use of such a powerful and useful tool.

Anything considered adult-oriented, offensive, illegal, malicious, or possibly questionable as deemed by either the *Parent Name* or *Child Name* should be exited immediately and discussed. Any time an inappropriate site or content is accessed on the computer, even if by accident, *Child Name* must report it to *Parent Name*.

E-mail correspondence should always be polite, nonoffensive, using appropriate language. *Never* reveal private information about our last name, where we live, our phone number, address, or city location to nonfamily members on the Internet. Do not share personal details or thoughts with anyone on the Internet unless approved by *Parent Name* for something like an e-mail to a family member.

Consequences

Parent Name will consider the appropriate restrictions for each offense listed below:

1. If the computer is not operated correctly, with neglect or misuse, access to the computer will be denied.

2. If the Internet is used to access inappropriate material, access to the Internet will be denied.

3. If Internet browser history is deleted by the child, access to the Internet will be denied.

4. If filtering or security software is disabled, access to the computer will be denied.

Child Signature   Date

Parent Signature   Date

Backing Up Data

As soon as you lose that big report to the boss, or the paper for your final project in a class, you realize the extreme importance of backing up data! System administrators in corporations need to back up data on a regular basis using automated tools such as tape backup and mirroring drives on a server. Workstation or home users also need to back up data on a regular basis. As a general rule, I back up all important files after making major updates.

Back up data often

Backing up data should be done often to avoid problems with data recovery. For example, if data on a network is only backed up once a week on a tape drive users can lose up to 7 days of work in a worst-case scenario. Backing up work to a tape drive nightly only puts at risk 24 hours of work.

When backing up data, consider all types, including standard files authored in programs like Microsoft Office and Internet browser favorites, Outlook files, Office templates, computer registry, and more. Other important files often overlooked during the backup process include `config.sys`, `autoexec.bat`, `win.ini`, and `system.ini`. These files should be backed up each time a change is made to the system, including installation of new software.

Programs like Microsoft Word offer auto-backup options that users may want to make use of on a regular basis. Microsoft Word supports at least three backup options, versions, backup saves, and AutoRecover.

To make use of versions, select Versions... from the File menu and click on the Save Now... button to save a copy of the current document. A checkbox for automatically saving versions every time a file is closed is also available. To access a backup version at a later date, simply select Versions... from the File menu again and select the file of interest. When an older version is opened, Microsoft Word automatically displays the older version as a read-only file, tiling open windows. If the auto-save option for Versions is used, it's a good idea to delete extra versions from time to time to avoid large file sizes.

To make use of both backup saves and auto-recovery in Microsoft Word select Options... from the Tools menu and click on the Save tab. Add a checkmark next to Always create a backup copy to have Microsoft Word save backups automatically while a user works on a file. Add a checkmark next to Save AutoRecover info every: to create AutoRecover documents as often as desired. Performance lags may be experienced with both of these options selected, as Microsoft Word saves files in the background.

After backing up files, consider keeping an extra copy offsite. If a fire or other disaster occurs, the offsite copy may be used to restore lost files quickly. Because of time and expense, offsite backup is most often done with master archive files on a less regular basis.

Types of backup options

There are several backup methods that may be employed, each with distinct benefits. Backing up files often, especially in a corporate environment, is essential. Consider using several backup methods to best protect network data. Also consider backing up "backup" and other essential programs, in case an entire drive is destroyed during a malware attack.

Automated backups take place at regular intervals, backing up files as configured. Some backup programs only backup files that have changed since the last backup, rather than backing up all files in a given directory. This places only one copy of a given document on a backup disk or file. If that single disk or file happens to be corrupt, the backup file may be lost. Backing up multiple copies of files, over a period of days, provides much better protection.

Compressed backups are files that are backed up in a separate compressed file, such as a ZIP file. To make use of a compressed backup, files must be decompressed. Compression is also an option for mass storage devices, such as tape backups, enabling users to back up more data on a given tape when using compression.

Manual backup includes copying files to a floppy disk, CD ROM, or other media storage devices such as ZIP or JAZZ disks. Manually copying files can take a long time, especially when burning to a CD ROM. Also, users may forget to back up certain files that would not be missed with an automated backup program.

Some backup programs enable users to back up entire drives at a time, saved as a separate file on a local drive or other disk. Unfortunately, some programs do not enable users to restore individual files backed up with this method. If a single file is needed, an entire restoration of all files backed up may be required. If such a program is being used, users should make sure that they back up files individually to disk as well.

One tip for users who wish to incrementally back up manually recently changed files is to use an advanced feature of the `Find` tool on Windows 95/98 operating systems. Select `Files or Folders` from the `Find` menu located under the `Start` menu to access the `Find` tool. Select a location to search, such as the C drive on the computer, and click on the Date tab. Click on Find all files and then between to enter a date range, as shown in Figure 5.6. Click on Find Now to initiate a search that will find all files modified within the date range and drive selected. After a list is generated by the Find tool, click on Type to organize the list. Then select and drag copies of modified files to a disk to manually back them up.

Risks of reinfection from backups

If a virus is detected and removed from a system it may also reside on recent backups. An important virus-removal step is to scan and remove viruses from all media, especially floppy disks, e-mails, and backup files.

Some antivirus programs have difficulty detecting and removing viruses from password-protected or compressed archives. If a virus is found on a system, decompressing files and analyzing them for viruses may help avoid reinfection at a later date.

Network administrators normally overwrite tapes every few weeks. If an outbreak occurs on the network, they may want to simply label a backup disk as possi-

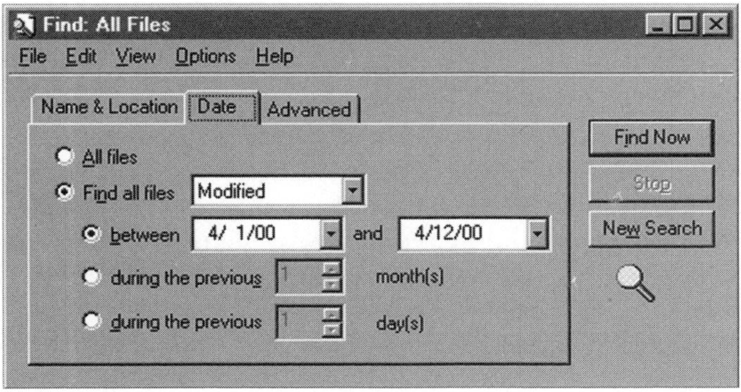

Figure 5.6 Using Find to locate recently modified files.

bly infected, to make sure it's scanned for viruses if files are retrieved from the tape prior to overwriting the tape.

Benefits of backup when infected

Backing up essential files, especially when a virus is detected on a system, may help recover files infected with a virus. Any backup made in such a situation should be labeled something like "Infected—Use with Caution." After successfully removing the virus from the system, check to see that all files work correctly and are not damaged.

If files are found to be damaged, use the infected backup file and different removal techniques to attempt to save the file while removing the virus. Using a different antivirus program will sometimes work better, removing a virus without damaging the infected file. See Section 7 on removing viruses for more ideas on how to rescue infected files.

Updates and Upgrades to Antivirus Software

Upgrades refer to program enhancements and improvements made to a software program. Updates refer to small fixes or updates made on a regular basis to something like a virus string's database file. Having both updated and upgraded software helps a user to obtain the best possible protection with a given antivirus software program.

Benefits of upgrades

Upgrades often provide improved performance, easier-to-use controls and interface, and new functionality. As a general rule, antivirus programs should be upgraded about every year or when a major upgrade is made available. Upgrades can become very important to a user when it helps to avoid negative effects on a computing environment, such as the year 2000 upgrades recently acquired by many computer users.

Benefits of updating software often

Updating the virus strings database file for an antivirus program on a regular basis is an important routine to establish as soon as a computer is acquired. Home users may want to update less frequently to take the hassle out of antivirus scanning when they don't use their computer for essential or important functions. Users that make use of their computer for business, professional, or other important functions should update frequently, such as weekly (if not daily).

Various antivirus programs support different types of virus strings database downloads through the Internet. Some require that large, complete downloads take place for any given virus strings database file. Others enable users to download small temporary patches and then perform a periodic update over time. When considering an antivirus program be sure to look into how big the average update is, how often updates are made available, and how easily updates may be obtained from the company.

Most antivirus companies have Internet Web pages available for downloading updates. Updates fall under a host of names, several of which are identified in Table 5.2.

The ease of updating and cost of updates (if any) are important considerations for some users when selecting an antivirus product. Many companies are working to make the update process even easier by incorporating point and click and automated updated features within antivirus software. Going one step further, companies like McAfee and Trend Micro, Inc., now offer online scanning tools, requiring no local installation of software.

The advantage to using online scanning tools is that users don't have to configure, update, or manage any software on their machine. Users simply point their Internet browser to the appropriate location to run a scan of files on their hard drive. While this method works great for home and small business users, it cur-

TABLE 5.2
Virus strings database file names

Update Names	
Alwil	Signature
Computer Associates	Signature
F-Prot	Sign.def and Macro.def
F-Secure	Definition
McAfee VirusScan	DAT
Norman Virus Control	DEF
Sophos Antivirus	IDE
Symantec Corporation, Inc.	Virus Definitions
Trend Micro Systems, Inc.	Virus Pattern

rently has serious limitations and considerations for secure corporate environments.

Alternative Operating Systems and Programs

DOS and Windows 3.X/95/98/2000 are commonly attacked operating systems (OS). In contrast, the Linux OS is a popular choice as a corporate gateway antivirus scanning solution since it has few OS specific attacks in existence at the time of writing this book. Other platforms also enjoy few OS specific viruses, including Unix, SunOS, and Macintosh. Macintosh OS 7.X and newer have even fewer Macintosh OS specific viruses. Unfortunately, some threats cross the boundaries of being OS specific, such as Internet threats and macro viruses that function in Microsoft Word on both Macintosh and Windows OS.

Alternative programs

WordPerfect and ClarisWorks (Macintosh) are popular alternatives to Microsoft Word and are not subject to cross-platform macro viruses. Simply selecting a different word processing program can effectively remove the threat of macro viruses!

WordPad and NotePad on a PC, and TeachText on a Macintosh, are alternatives to Microsoft Word. Unfortunately, these programs do not support the same powerful features as Microsoft Word.

Alternative file types

As a user of Microsoft Word or programs mentioned previously, a user can easily save and transfer data without the threat of macro viruses. To create an alternative file type, use the Save As... feature in Microsoft Word or use a program that supports the creation of the file type desired. Figure 5.7 illustrates a file being saved in rich text format to lower the threat of macro viruses.

ASCII (plain) text files, commonly created with Microsoft Word or NotePad, support text with minimal formatting. WordPad documents support some intermediate format features along with text font, style, size, color, and pictures. Rich text files support standard Microsoft Word features but do not support macros.

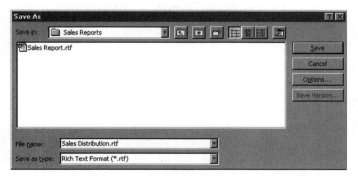

Figure 5.7 Using Save As... in Microsoft Word to create a rich text format file.

Saving files as an Internet Web page, in HTML format, is another way to distribute and send files to others.

Tricks and Techniques

A variety of helpful tips and techniques, some of which are reviewed elsewhere in this book, are provided in this section. Use the following tips and techniques to improve system performance, avoid malware infections, and better manage infections if they occur.

Use Scandisk and defragment utilities

Newer versions of Windows include Scandisk and defragment utilities that every user should run on a regular basis. Scandisk is able to fix errors on a drive, free up lost file fragments, and manage invalid data. Scandisk may also remove ghost files that are left after removal of a virus from a system. Older versions of PC operating systems, including DOS, may use CHKDSK /F to "fix" files on a drive if Scandisk is not available.

Defragmenting optimizes a drive for performance and frees up space on a drive. Defragmenting should be performed often on machines with lots of files being copied, created, and then deleted on a regular basis. The more file management that occurs on a machine, the more fragmented it becomes over time. Defragmenting is especially useful when space on a hard drive becomes limited or performance issues arise on a system due to heavy fragmentation of a disk.

If you're not able to find Scandisk or a defragmenting utility on your machine, use the Run... box located under the Start menu to enter Scandisk or defrag and press Enter to run the program.

Other commercial solutions are also available and recommended for serious computer users, such as Norton Utilities, to back up, repair, and manage files and fragmentation on disks.

Use MSCONFIG to back up system files

On supported PC computers, type `msconfig` into the `Run...` box, located under the `Start` menu, to run the system configuration utility. Click on the `Create Backup` button to create a backup on the hard disk of important files such as `config.sys` and `win.ini`. Use `MSCONFIG` to easily troubleshoot and edit various system files, avoiding typos and other common errors when troubleshooting such files manually.

Cloning setup for fast network repairs/images

Using imaging programs like Ghost gives network administrators an easy way to clone (back up) common setup profiles and applications on a desktop. If serious damage occurs, the entire software setup may be quickly restored by extracting a backup image to the drive in question. Some imaging programs even allow partition data to be included in the image. Image files may be run through just about any media, including ZIP disks, CD ROM discs, or network connections.

A simple manual method is to compare two similar systems on a network, copying over files that are different on a system in question. Because multiple configuration and access issues commonly arise through complex rebuilding of a severely damaged system, this method is discouraged, especially for large corporations.

Saving files on a different partition or drive

Saving files to a different partition or drive may help to rescue files, especially when the operating system needs to be reinstalled. Several malware programs specifically attack the `C` drive, the normal drive letter assigned to the main partition of a hard drive containing the operating system and other important software.

By installing programs on the C drive and data files on a different partition or drive, they may be more easily protected and rescued. For example, if Windows becomes corrupt it may be reinstalled without any loss of data on a separate partition or drive. C drive–specific data that may be lost is minimal, only loosing items such as Office templates, Outlook data, and Internet Explorer favorites that are not backed up on a different drive. All other data stored on a different partition or disk is reasonably protected from becoming corrupted or overwritten during a reinstallation of the operating system to the C drive.

BIOS options

Several BIOS options may help lower the risk of virus infections on a system: disabling the floppy drive if it is not needed on a system, changing the boot order to start up from the hard drive first, and password-protecting the system. Press the appropriate key during startup, such as Delete or F2, to change BIOS options as desired. Reboot the computer and verify changes made to the BIOS. For example, if the boot order has been changed, insert a clean floppy disk and see if the system boots from the hard drive instead of the floppy disk, as configured in the BIOS.

Disabling files in recycle bin

When troubleshooting, it may help to disable files by moving them into the recycle bin, restarting, and testing a system. If functionality is negatively affected, the file in the recycle bin can easily be restored. Simply open the recycle bin and right-click on the file in question to select Restore. The file is automatically restored to its original location on the drive. Reboot the machine and continue testing until troubleshooting is complete.

If the file does not negatively affect functionality, continue troubleshooting. After questionable files have been tested, back them up on a disk, from the recycle bin, and empty the recycle bin when done. Label the disk appropriately and secure it in a safe location. If a questionable file is needed in the future, it will still be available on disk.

File attributes

Changing file attributes to something like read-only helps to protect a file from unwanted changes and infection. In DOS, use the `ATTRIB +R` command and switch to create read-only files. In Windows 98 simply

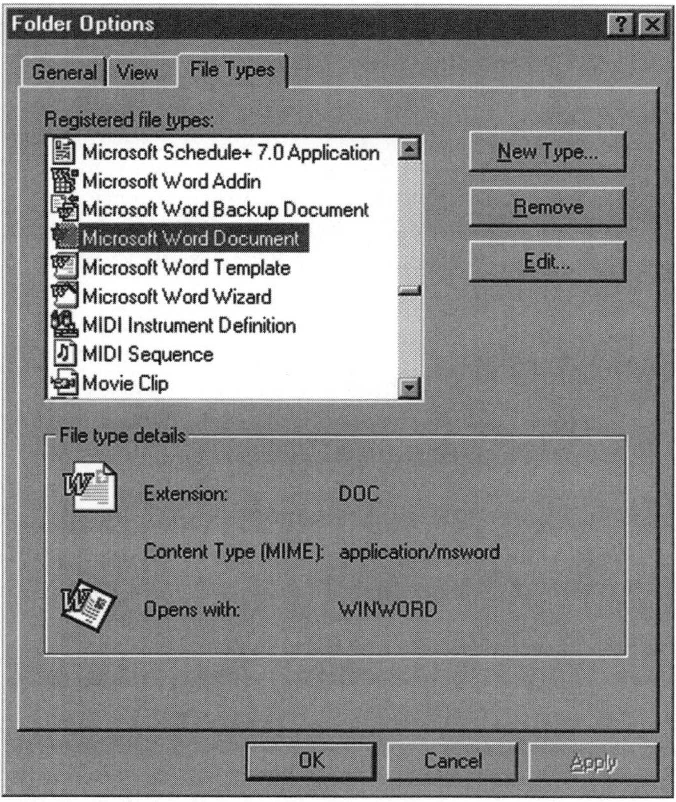

Figure 5.8 Changing Windows 98 file associations.

right-click on a document, select `Properties`, and add a check in the `Read-only` checkmark box. A time-saving tip is to select multiple files at once with shift-click, control-click, or click and drag, and then right-click on the group to set read-only properties for each selected file. Folders may also be set to read-only.

Restricting read and write privileges on a network may help to avoid or slow down infections across the network. For example, a workstation could become infected by a file-infecting virus. Network files, located in a read-only directory on the network, will not be infected by a virus since "write" privileges are not enabled.

Locking a 3.5-in floppy disk

Lock high-density 3.5-in floppy disks by moving the plastic tab up so that a hole can be seen through the disk container. Once a disk is locked, malware may not make changes to the disk, preventing infection. For this reason, emergency, boot, and antivirus disks should always be locked after creation to keep them free of malware.

If a disk needs to be updated at a later time, simply move the tab down and insert into the computer. On disks without a tab, which is sometimes removed with free-marketed disks, simply place tape over the hole to enable write access. Unfortunately, users sometimes do this inadvertently with a disk label, covering the locked hole on a 3.5-in floppy disk. The result is that the disk is not locked, since light is not able to shine through the hole in the disk. If light is able to shine through the hole, it is seen as locked and will not be changed by any software event.

Changing file associations

Avoid macro viruses by changing file associations to automatically load Microsoft Word files in a different program that does not support macros, such as

NotePad. Add an option to edit files with Word, making it easy to right-click on a file and open it with Word. Otherwise the simple double-click action loads all Microsoft Word files in the new default application associated with the file type.

To change file associations in Windows 98 open My Computer and select Folder Options... from the View menu. Click on the File Types menu and locate files of interest, such as Microsoft Word documents and templates. Click on the file of interest and then click on the Edit... button, as shown in Figure 5.8.

Click on the bold Open option and click on Edit to browse for a new target link. Click on the Browse... button to locate the new program, such as NotePad, to link to when such a file is opened and click on OK. To add an editing item, either edit an existing option or click on New... and enter a name and browse for a link to a program of interest, such as Microsoft Word.

Password protect `normal.dot`

Password protecting the normal Microsoft Word file helps to guard against future macro virus infections. If anything attempts to modify the protected file, a prompt for a password blocks the action and alerts the user.

1. Delete normal.dot (normal on a Macintosh) to force Microsoft Word to create a new file. This file is normally located within the Templates directory of the Microsoft Office folder on the hard drive.

2. Run Microsoft Word.

3. Press ALT-F11 to open the Visual Basic editor on a PC or select the editor from the Macros sub-menu of the Tools menu.

4. Select Project Explorer from the View menu and click on normal.dot.

5. Select Normal Properties from the Tools menu and click on the Protection tab.

6. Check the `Lock project for viewing` and enter a password. Write down the password and store it in a safe place.

7. Select `Save` from the `File` menu and then `Close` the Visual Basic editor to return to Microsoft Windows.

Compressing executables

Compressing files, especially executables, may help to avoid virus attempts to infect or spread through a system. For example, an application infecting virus may skip over `.sit`, `.hqx`, or `.zip` files when looking for an application to infect. Compressing files and programs that are not often used also saves disk space and may be automated by a commercial program.

Opening files in NotePad or Quick View

Opening a Microsoft Word file in NotePad poses no threat of macro virus infection. NotePad does not recognize or support macros in any way. Simply save new Word files or e-mail attachments to the hard drive, run NotePad, and open Microsoft Word files of interest (in NotePad) to view the text contents. Another option is to right-click on saved files to select `Quick View`. Both methods for viewing files, especially Microsoft Word files, are fairly safe and effective.

Fitting F-Prot on a floppy disk

After downloading F-Prot and updated `sign.def` and `macro.def` files, consider creating a floppy disk with F-Prot. If a virus infects the computer at a later date, the computer may be booted from a clean, locked floppy and disinfected with F-Prot running off of a floppy disk.

Because F-Prot has grown in size, the `macro.def` file can no longer fit on a standard 3.5-in floppy disk. The workaround is to create a dummy `macro.def` file to enable F-Prot to run, scanning all types of viruses other than macro viruses. Place a working copy of F-Prot on a disk by following the instructions below:

1. Obtain a newly reformatted or preformatted 3.5-in floppy disk.

2. Copy `F-Prot.EXE`, `English.TXO`, `Sign.def`, `Sign2.def`, and `nomacro.def` to the disk.

3. Rename `nomacro.def` to `macro.def`.

After running a scan with F-Prot off of disk, the computer may be rebooted from the hard disk. Then run a full version of F-Prot (including `macro.def`), from the hard drive, to detect and remove any macro viruses in memory.

Create new boot and emergency disk with updates

Whenever an update or upgrade is done on a computer it's a good idea to create new boot and emergency disks. Having the exact same version of DOS on a boot disk is essential for some operations, requiring users to create new boot disks each time the operating system is updated (at a minimum). Keep old boot and emergency disks stored away in a safe place, using them as a backup in case the new disks end up becoming infected or corrupted for some reason.

Fdisk

Fdisk is a DOS utility that enables expert users to work with the master boot record of a hard disk. Some users like to use Fdisk to remove viruses from the master boot record. Because information in the master boot record is not reformatted with a drive, some users falsely believe that some viruses may not be removed from a computer.

Fdisk must be used with caution, by *expert users only*, to avoid wiping out an entire drive! Do *not* use

Fdisk when viruses like Monkey and One_Half have infected the system. Monkey does not preserve the partition table and One_Half stores a decryption key in the master boot record. Also avoid using Fdisk when disk managers such as EZDrive are installed on the computer.

To remove a master boot record virus users can simply start up the computer from a clean boot disk and use antivirus software or use Fdisk, run from a clean disk. To use Fdisk enter the following command from the DOS prompt to remove a virus from the master boot record; FDISK /MBR. For more help on Fdisk attempt to load DOS help by entering FDISK /?, FDISK HELP, or HELP.

Restart for second scan

Shut down, turn off the computer for about 30 seconds, and restart a computer to scan with a second on-demand antivirus program. Sometimes information stored in RAM from the first antivirus program scan job may adversely affect scanning completed by the second program. This is especially important if two different antivirus programs render conflicting results with one another.

Use passwords

Make use of passwords on the BIOS, Windows login, compressed files, screen saver, Microsoft Word files, and other areas supported with password protection to increase the overall security of data on a computer. Avoid setting passwords that are easy to hack. When setting more than one password on a system, use different passwords for each program.

To see if a program supports passwords, look for words like password, protect, and security within the menus or help file. For example, to set a password in the BIOS press the appropriate key during startup, such as `Delete` or `F2`, and look for password-related items in the CMOS.

Passwords are sometimes discouraged in a corporate environment since setting a password restricts access to a file. Avoid access issues by writing down all passwords on a "password log" sheet, securing the paper to avoid security issues. If a password is forgotten, the password log sheet can be a lifesaver.

Locking the HyperCard Home stack

Locking the Home stack of HyperCard on a Macintosh is a great way to prevent changes made to the Home stack script. Common HyperCard viruses, such as Merryxmas and Wormcode, spread by inserting a copy of the virus into the Home stack script. If the stack is locked, changes can't be made. The Home stack can be locked two different ways, in HyperCard and also in the Finder.

In HyperCard select `Protect...` from the `File` menu to update the protection settings for HyperCard. Add checkmarks to items of interest, including `Can't Modify Stack` and `Can't Delete Stack`, as shown in Figure 5.9. If HyperCard is used by more than one individual, consider clicking on `Set Password...` to password-protect options selected. After clicking on `OK`, the Home stack is reasonably protected. However, scripts are able to change these settings, so locking the Home stack in the Finder is also important.

Quit HyperCard or HyperCard Player if open and locate the application(s) on the computer (Finder). Click on the Home stack once to select it. Press `Command-I` or select `Get Info...` from the `File` menu to display the Information box for the Home stack. Add a checkmark to the `Locked` option in the lower-left corner to lock the Home stack as shown in Figure 5.10.

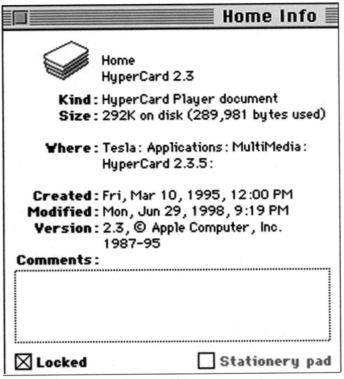

Figure 5.9 Protecting the Home stack to prevent infection.

HyperCard inoculation script

Several HyperCard virus families are easily protected against by inserting an inoculation script in the Home stack of HyperCard and HyperCard Player on Macintosh computers. At the very end of the HyperCard Home stack script insert Jacque Landman Gay's inoculation script as shown below to protect against Pickle, Blink, Independence Day, Merryxmas, Merry2xmas, Lopez, Crudshot, Merryxmas Antibody, and Wormcode (copy exactly as shown).

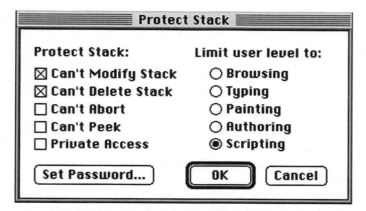

Figure 5.10 Locking the Home stack script to prevent infection.

```
-- if the script of home contains -- pickle
--    -- blink [Option-7, the paragraph sign]
-- Independance Day -- Independance Day (sic)
--on idle --merryxmas
--on openbackground --merryxmas
--on closebackground --merryxmas
--on idle --merry2xmas
--on openbackground --merry2xmas
--on closebackground --merry2xmas
--on idle --Lopez
--on openbackground --Lopez
--on closebackground --Lopez
--on idle --crudshot
--on openbackground --crudshot
--on closebackground --crudshot
--on openstack --merryxmas antibody
-- THE FOLLOWING LINE FOR WORMCODE MUST
-- REMAIN LAST, WITH NO LEADING HYPHENS:
end openstack --home script 2
```

Some antivirus programs may detect the inoculation script as a virus, even though it is not a virus. This happens when an antivirus developer does make a distinction between actual viruses and inoculation scripts that are similar to strings found in actual viruses. If an antivirus program does detect the script as a virus, it's important to check the Home stack script to make sure the inoculation script was not removed. If it was removed, consider changing the settings of the antivirus program in question, obtaining a different antivirus program, or not using the inoculation script protection option.

HyperCard Set Script Trap

Using Jacque Landman Gay's Set Script Trap enables a HyperCard user to monitor the activity of HyperCard. If a HyperCard stack is unlocked, it may be changed by the user during an upgrade, installation, or a virus. The `set` command is used to update and save changes made to the Home stack script. Jacque Landman Gay's Set Script Trap does a wonderful job of intercepting all set script messages, enabling the user to allow or reject attempts made by HyperCard to change the Home stack script. Enter the set script handler into the Home stack script, as shown below (exactly) and save the Home stack script.

```
on set -- virus block
    if param(1) = "script" and param(3) contains "home" then
        answer "Another stack is attempting to alter"¬
        && " the script of the Home stack. Allow alteration?"¬
        with "Allow" or "Don't Allow"
        if it = "allow" then pass set
        else
            put "Home stack script has not been altered."¬
            && "Current handler has been aborted." into prompt
            if the userlevel = 5
          then put " Edit script of current stack?" after prompt
            if the userlevel < 5 then answer prompt
            else answer prompt with "Cancel" or "Edit"
            if it = "Cancel" then exit to HyperCard
          edit script of this stack -- allows removal of virus
            exit to HyperCard
        end if
    else pass set
end set
```

Antivirus Software

Selection of antivirus software solutions depends upon many factors, including robustness, computing environment, value of data stored or processed on a computer, expense, ease of use, customizable features, available support, and more.

Arguably, the most important feature of antivirus software is its ability to detect and remove 100 percent of all viruses In the Wild. Although no program can offer 100 percent protection all the time, there are some great packages that consistently deliver high-quality results. Reference third-party reviews to identify which antivirus products, for various operating systems, consistently detect and remove known viruses In the Wild at the time of testing. Over time various vendors and antivirus packages for specific operating systems develop a clear track record of malware detection and removal performance.

Third-Party Reviews

ICSA.net, Virus Bulletin, West Coast Labs, HackFix, Virus Test Center certifications, and other reviews of commercial antivirus programs are great indicators of which programs are the most robust, able to detect and remove malware In the Wild. Each organization has a unique testing method, performed at various times of the calendar year.

Reviews included here are good guidelines at the time of writing this book. Because third-party tests are ongoing, correlate current online information with test results provided in this book. Comparing results enable users to identify which programs consistently provide the best protection available for a specific operating system.

Comparing several test results over a period of time also helps to avoid date-specific interpretation issues, where a single test may not always best reflect the capabilities of a program. For example, if testing is completed just a few days before an update to a program is made, detection and removal results may not best reflect the overall long-term performance of a given product.

ICSA.net Certification

ICSA.net, publishers of *Information Security* magazine, certifies products on a quarterly basis (at a minimum) for the ability to detect and remove viruses In the Wild. Table 6.1 identifies ICSA.net certified products, referenced at http://www.icsa.net/, as of May 2000.

E-mail gateways are also certified by ICSA.net, identified in Table 6.2.

Virus Bulletin 100 percent Awards

Virus Bulletin, an industry leader at http://www.virus-btn.com, has identified antivirus products that they feel are best able to detect known viruses In the Wild. Unlike some tests, Virus Bulletin uses a recently updated list of viruses In the Wild to test software for the 100 percent award. Some longitudinal data is available, dating back several months, as shown in Table 6.3, for selected 100 percent awards (recent).

TABLE 6.1
USCA.net Certified Antivirus Programs as of Year 2000

Computer Associates	InoculateIT Personal Edition for Windows 95/98. InoculateIT Antivirus for Windows 95/98, NT Server, and NetWare. InoculateIT for Windows 2000.
Command Software	Command Antivirus for Windows 95/98.
Panda Software	Panda Antivirus for Windows 95/98/2000, NT Server, and NetWare.
Symantec	Norton AntiVirus for Windows 3.X/95/98/2000, NT Workstation, NT Server, and NetWare. Norton AntiVirus Corporate Edition for Windows 2000.
Trend Micro	PC-cillin for Windows 95/98, NT Workstation. OfficeScan for Windows 95/98, NT Workstation Server Protect for Windows NT and NetWare.

TABLE 6.2
ICSA.net Certified E-mail Gateways as of May 2000

Aladdin	eSafe Protect Gateway.
Symantec	Norton AntiVirus for Internet E-mail Gateways.
Trend Micro	InterScan VirusWall.

Tests are completed on a single operating system for each month.

Programs that regularly receive the 100 percent award for a given operating system have a good reliability track record. Table 6.4 identifies consistent programs based upon 100 percent awards listed in Table 6.3.

Although the Virus Bulletin 100 percent detection capability is important, the ability for an antivirus program to remove a detected virus is a different issue.

TABLE 6.3
Virus Bulletin 100 percent Awards

Windows NT April 2000	Vet Anti-Virus v10.1.7.1 NOD32 v1.31 F-Secure Anti-Virus v5.02.5528 AVP v3.0.132.4 Sophos Anti-Virus v3.30 Norton AntiVirus 2000 v6.00.03
DOS February 2000	Vet Anti-Virus 1/11/99 Command AntiVirus v4.57.4 Dialog Science DrWeb v4.14 NOD32 v1.27 FRISK Software F-Prot 3.06a AVG v6.087 AVP v3.0.132 VirusScan v4.0.4.4049 Virus Control v4.72 Sophos Anti-Virus v3.27 Norton Antivirus 25/10/99
DOS January 2000	F-Secure Anti-Virus 2.0.125 NOD32 v1.11 iRiS AntiVirus v22.14 AVP v3.0.125 VirusScan v4.0.4.4001 Virus Control v4.72 Sophos Anti-Virus v3.15 Norton Antivirus v4.0
Windows 98 November 1999	Vet Anti-Virus v10.1.0 Command AntiVirus v4.57 DrWeb v4.12a NOD32 v1.24 RAV v7.0 AVP v3.0.131 Virus Control v4.72 Norton Antivirus v5.02.04
Windows 98 November 1998	AVAST32 v7.70 Inoculan v5.0.4 F-Secure Anti-Virus 4.02 NOD32 v1.09 iRiS AntiVirus v22.13 AVP v3.0 Dr Solomon AVTK v7.87 Virus Control v4.52 Sophos Anti-Virus v3.13 Norton Antivirus v5.00.01

TABLE 6.3
Virus Bulletin 100 percent Awards (*Continued*)

Windows NT September 1999	InnoculateIT v4.53 Vet Anti-Virus v10.0.2 NOD32 v1.20 RAV v7.0 AVP v3.0.131 Virus Control v4.70
Windows NT March 1999	NOD32 v1.13 iRiS AntiVirus v22.16 AVP v3.0.131 NetShield NT v4.0.2.4008 Virus Control v4.63 Sophos Anti-Virus v3.17
NetWare July 1999	InnoculateIT v4.5 Norton Antivirus v4.04

TABLE 6.4
Consistent Virus Bulletin 100 percent
Detection Certified Products by
Operating System

Consistent Programs	
DOS	NOD32 AVP VirusScan Virus Control Sophos Anti-Virus Norton Antivirus
Windows 98	NOD32 AVP Virus Control Norton Antivirus
Windows NT	NOD32 AVP Virus Control Sophos Anti-Virus
NetWare	InnoculateIT Norton Antivirus

West Coast Labs has developed tests for both detection as well as removal abilities of antivirus programs for viruses and Trojans In the Wild.

West Coast Labs Test Results

West Coast Labs, at http://www.check-mark.com/, independently tests antivirus programs for their ability to detect and remove viruses and Trojans In the Wild. If a program is certified at "checkmark level 1," it is able to detect 100 percent of all viruses In the Wild at the time of testing. Table 6.5 lists antivirus programs that are checkmark level 1 as of May 2000.

Level 2 certification requires that the antivirus program is able to detect 100 percent of the viruses In the Wild and successfully remove them from the system without damaging side effects. Table 6.6 lists antivirus programs that are checkmark level 2 as of May 2000.

West Coast Labs has more recently developed a Trojan Checkmark for antivirus programs that are able to detect Trojans contained within the West Coast Labs Trojan test suite. Table 6.7 lists antivirus programs that are Trojan checkmark certified as of May 2000.

If a user is most interested in using a program that is able to detect and remove viruses and Trojans In the Wild, referencing both checkmark level 2 and Trojan checkmark programs provides the best lab measurements for antivirus protection. Programs that are the most robust, certified for level 1, level 2, and Trojan certification, are identified in Table 6.8.

HackFix Findings

HackFix, at http://www.hackfix.org/hackfix/, is a non-profit volunteer organization that specializes in anti-Trojan efforts. One set of findings posted on the HackFix site in March 2000, summarized in Table 6.9, identifies the ability for antivirus programs to detect 94 older and obscure Trojans (various versions) in existence at the time of testing. Findings do not indicate

TABLE 6.5
Checkmark Level 1–Certified Antivirus Programs as of May 2000

Aladdin Knowledge Systems	ESafe Protect Enterprise for Windows 95/98
Command Software Systems	Anti-Virus for Windows NT Server, Workstation, 98, 95
Computer Associates	InoculateIT for Windows NT Workstation, 98, 95
F-Secure Corporation	F-Secure for Windows 95
eSafe	eSafe Protect Desktop for Windows NT Workstation, 98, 95
InDefense	InDefense for Windows NT Workstation, 98, 95
Kaspersky Labs	AVP for Windows NT Workstation, 98
Network Associates	NetShield for Windows 2000, NT Server, NetWare VirusScan for Windows NT Workstation, 98, 2000 GroupShield for Exchange and Lotus Notes
Norman Data Defense	Virus Control for Windows NT Workstation, 98, OS/2
Systems UK Ltd	Firebreak for NetWare
Panda Software International	Panda Anti-Virus for Windows NT Workstation, 3.X, OS/2, Exchange, DOS Panda Anti-Virus Platinum for Windows 98, 95 Administrator for Windows NT Server and NetWare
Symantec Inc.	Norton Anti-Virus for Windows NT Server, NetWare, 2000, 98, 95, DOS, OS/2
Trend Micro, Inc.	OfficeScan for Windows NT Workstation, 98, 95 ServerProtect for Windows NT Server, NetWare ScanMail for Exchange

Table 6.6
Checkmark Level 2–Certified Antivirus Programs as of May 2000

Command Software Systems	Anti-Virus for Windows NT Server, Workstation, 98, 95
Computer Associates	InoculateIT for Windows NT Workstation, 98, 95, 3.X Cheyenne Antivirus for Windows 98
F-Secure Corporation	F-Secure for Windows 95
Kaspersky Labs	AVP for Windows 98
Network Associates	VirusScan for Windows 98 and 2000 Professional
	NetShield for Windows NT Server and 2000 Server GroupShield for Lotus Notes
Panda Software International	Panda Anti-Virus Platinum for Windows 98, 95 Panda Anti-Virus for NetWare and Exchange
Symantec Inc.	Norton Anti-Virus for Windows NT Server, Workstation, NetWare, 2000 Professional, 2000 Server, Lotus Notes, 98, 95, DOS, and OS/2
Trend Micro, Inc.	OfficeScan for Windows 98

the ability for an antivirus program to remove detected malware.

For Trojan detection, PC-cillin (93%) and Antivirus Toolkit Pro (74%) are the clear leaders in this set of findings. Norton Antivirus is the least-effective Trojan detection tool, failing to detect 64% of Trojans tested.

Virus Test Center (VTC)— University of Hamburg

VTC performs a variety of detailed tests of antivirus software, with results posted at http://agn-www.informatik.uni-hamburg.de/vtc/naveng.htm. A recent VTC test, Millennium Test 2000-02, was completed on

Table 6.7
Trojan Checkmark Certified Antivirus Programs as of May 2000

Trojan Checkmark	
Computer Associates	InoculateIT for Windows NT Workstation and 98
F-Secure Corporation	F-Secure for Windows 95
Kaspersky Lab	AVP for Windows NT Workstation and 98
Network Associates	VirusScan for Windows NT Workstation and 95
Panda Software International	Panda Anti-Virus for Windows 95 and 3.X
	Panda AntiVirus Pro for Windows NT Workstation
Symantec Inc.	Norton Anti-Virus for Windows NT Server, Workstation, 98, and 3.X
Trend Micro, Inc.	OfficeScan for Windows NT Workstation, 95 ScanMail for Exchange

Table 6.8
Robust Antivirus Programs as Correlated by West Coast Labs Data, May 2000

Computer Associates	InoculateIT for Windows NT Workstation, 98
F-Secure Corporation	F-Secure for Windows 95
Kaspersky Lab	AVP for Windows 98
Panda Software International	Panda Anti-Virus for Windows 95
Symantec Inc.	Norton Anti-Virus for Windows NT Server, Workstation, 98, 3.X

February 26, 2000, and updated March 1, 2000. Results for detection capabilities of DOS antivirus programs are listed in Table 6.10. See the Internet site for additional details and other test data.

Table 6.9
Antivirus Programs Able to Detect Old and Obscure Trojans According to HackFix Findings, March 2000

Antivirus Program	Detects ALL Versions of Trojan	Detects Some Versions of Trojan	Does *not* detect any Version of Trojan
Antivirus Toolkit Pro (AVP)	74%—70 of 94	7%—7 of 94	18%—17 of 94
Norton Antivirus	20%—19 of 94	16%—15 of 94	64%—60 of 94
McAfee Antivirus	34%—32 of 94	17%—16 of 94	49%—46 of 94
PC-cillin	93%—87 of 94	2%—2 of 94	5%—5 of 94
InoculateIT PE	30%—28 of 94	12%—11 of 94	59%—55 of 94

Table 6.10
VTC Test Results for DOS Antivirus Software as of March 1, 2000

Detection Test	DOS Antivirus
Detects 100% of Zoo Viruses	Command Software Antivirus, F-Prot, McAfee VirusScan
Detects 100% of In the Wild Viruses	Antivirus Toolkit Pro, Command Software Antivirus, DrWeb, F-Prot, FSAV, InocuLAN, NOD, Norman Virus Control, PAV, Sweep

Internet Downloads and Trialware

Internet users can quickly download a wide variety of antivirus solutions to use for free or test before deciding to purchase a program. Most commercial programs offer "trialware," where the user is able to "try before you buy." Updates and upgrades to commercial programs are also available through the Internet.

"Quick-fix" programs are less comprehensive, detecting and removing individual malware, such as Wormfood, that only detects and removes the Autostart worm. Programs like this can be very helpful when new malware is discovered In the Wild. Sometimes it takes a few days or weeks for antivirus developers to update virus strings databases. Using a quick-fix program, in the meanwhile, lowers the risk of infection. Quick-fix programs may not be very compatible or reliable and may require a higher level of user knowledge to use appropriately.

Free Antivirus Solutions

Contrary to what you might think, some of the best antivirus solutions are free! Qualifying the value of each freeware program, in conjunction with existing commercial solutions, is a great way to diversify antivirus protection on a computer.

Some programs are free for home users but not for corporate (nonprivate) users. F-Prot is a good example of a robust freeware application for home users. Although it is free for home users, corporate users must pay for a professional solution. There are only a handful of free PC antivirus programs that offer comprehensive solutions at the time of writing this book:

- InoculateIT Personal Edition (on-demand and on-access)
- F-Prot (on-demand)
- HouseCall (on-demand online scanner)
- VirusScan (on-demand online scanner)

Macintosh Antivirus Software

Macintosh users have few commercial antivirus options. Although some free programs do exist on the Macintosh, they do not protect against all three main categories of Macintosh viruses: Macintosh system viruses, HyperCard viruses, and macro viruses.

None of the third-party testing groups identified in this section includes Macintosh software test results. Of the few Macintosh-specific viruses that are In the Wild, few, if any, ever get posted on the predominantly PC-based WildList. The actual threat of Macintosh-specific viruses is somewhat vague and difficult to test since Macintosh malware is not as well explored as PC malware. Nevertheless, Macintosh users that use Microsoft Word and other Office products are susceptible to the same macro viruses that PC users face In the Wild.

Because there are so few Macintosh antivirus programs, overviews of products from Symantec, NAI, Sophos, and several shareware authors are provided below.

Norton Antivirus (formerly SAM) by Symantec

Recommended Price: $69.95

Requirements: Macintosh PowerPC processor, Mac OS 8.0 or greater, 24 MB of RAM, 10 MB of hard drive space, CD ROM drive, and an Internet connection for LiveUpdate.

NAV offers a user-friendly interface, quick scanning, powerful scan scheduling options, bloodhound heuristic technology, virus activation history, AppleGuide Help, SafeZone quarantine protection, and LiveUpdate for easy updating. NAV is now integrated with Norton Utilities, providing customers with outstanding data management, protection, and rescue utilities.

More information is available online at http://www.symantec.com/nav/nav_mac/.

Dr. Solomon Virex by NAI

Recommended Price: $49.95

Requirements: Macintosh OS 7.5.5 or greater, 4 MB of RAM, CD ROM drive preferred, and Internet access for easy updates.

Virex offers a user-friendly interface, drag and drop scanning with a control strip, scheduled scanning for Mac OS 8.X or greater users, and a powerful engine for scanning files (including compressed files). Network Associates, Inc., acquired both McAfee VirusScan and Dr. Solomon Antivirus in 1999, leading to the development of a single NAI Macintosh antivirus solution, Dr. Solomon's Virex.

More information is available online at http://www.mcafee.com/products/default.asp and http://www.mcafeeb2b.com/asp_set/products/tvd/virex_intro.sp.

Sophos Anti-Virus

Recommended Price: Varies

Requirements: Macintosh OS 7.0 or greater.

Sophos Anti-Virus, designed to work with network antivirus solutions, now provides support for Macintosh computers. Features include drag-and-drop testing, Virus Description Language (VDL) and SWEEP detection technology, automated update feature, quick on-access and on-demand scanning options, and centralized reporting.

More information is available online at http://www.sophos.com/products/antivirus/savmac.html.

Disinfectant

Recommended Price: Free

Requirements: System 7.X or greater.

This free and easy-to-use program is no longer developed but still useful to Macintosh users. This program detects and removes most Macintosh system–specific malware but does not protect against macro or HyperCard viruses.

An optional protection INIT enables Macintosh users to be protected while they work, running the on-demand scanner when desired. Damaged resource forks are also detected in scans, helping to avoid further corruption or file errors. An excellent encyclopedia of viruses is also included with Disinfectant.

Gatekeeper

Recommended Price: Free

Requirements: 128K ROM Macintosh processor, Macintosh OS 4.1 or greater (6.0.4 or greater preferred), and 512K RAM.

Gatekeeper is no longer developed but still provides Macintosh users with powerful protection against Macintosh-specific viruses. This program does not protect against macro or HyperCard viruses. Installation on Macintosh OS 7.0 or greater is easy—simply drag the three Gatekeeper externals over the top of the System folder and restart the computer. Access the Gatekeeper control panel after installation to customize protection options.

Merryxmas Vaccine

Recommended Price: Free

Requirements: HyperCard v2.1 or greater, color monitors preferred.

Still updated today, this popular freeware antivirus utility detects and removes blink, wormcode, merryxmas, merry2xmas, Lopez, and a few other HyperCard viruses. This on-demand scanner is easy to use and is updated periodically by Bill Swagerty, the author of the utility.

MerryxmasWatcher

Recommended Price: Free

Requirements: HyperCard 2.1 or greater.

Programmed by the author of this book, this utility is no longer being developed. This utility is still a popular HyperCard protection choice of Macintosh users today, eradicating and protecting against merryxmas and merry2xmas HyperCard viruses. The watcher script, installed in the Home stack, watches stacks while HyperCard is in use.

For additional Macintosh software protection options visit online sites such as About.com at http://antivirus.about.com/.

Antivirus Software Evaluation Form

Individual needs drive the focus of any formal software evaluation, covering a wide range of features available in various antivirus programs. Table 6.11 is a form that may be used to rank several different programs based upon criteria of interest. Select only the items of interest, ignoring extraneous features that are not important for individual needs.

Consider using a numeric system to rank items, such as scoring each item on a scale of 1 to 5, with 5

TABLE 6.11 Antivirus Software Evaluation Form

Features to Consider	Antivirus Program A	Antivirus Program B	Antivirus Program C
COST			
Street Price			
Rebates, if applicable			
Available Licenses for Home, Corporate, Site			
Updates to the Virus Strings Database			
Available Maintenance Agreements			
Length of Time for Free Updates (if available)			
Long-Term Expenses Incurred			
Upgrades to the Program			
Technical Support/Service			
Toll-Free or Charge Phone Line Service			
Warranty or Guarantee of Service/Performance			
Terms & Conditions			

Customer Training Expenses

SYSTEM REQUIREMENTS

Hardware Required

Operating Systems Supported

RAM Required

Hard Drive Space Required

Capable of Running from Floppy or CD ROM

INTERFACE & LEADERSHIP

Name Brand/Company

History

Progressive Solutions

Financially Sound

Strong Alliances in the Industry

User-friendly

Easy to Configure & Use

(Continued)

TABLE 6.11 Antivirus Software Evaluation Form (*Continued*)

Features to Consider	Antivirus Program A	Antivirus Program B	Antivirus Program C
Appealing Look & Feel			
Multiple Options for Tasks (menus, buttons, taskbar)			
Organized & Intuitive			
Languages Supported (English, Japanese, etc.)			
Installation			
Ease of Installation & Registration			
Quality of Installation Documentation			
Creates Emergency Boot Disk			
PERFORMANCE			
Reliability			
Stability			

Compatibility with Existing Programs on PC

Speed

Update/Upgrade Process

Automated or Manual

Ease of Installing

Frequency/Timely

Automated Reminder Notices

SCAN OPTIONS

On-Access

Command-Line

E-mail

On-Demand

Individual Files or Directories

Easy Access Such as Right-Click to Scan

Integrity Check

(*Continued*)

TABLE 6.11 Antivirus Software Evaluation Form (*Continued*)

Features to Consider	Antivirus Program A	Antivirus Program B	Antivirus Program C
Heuristics			
Accuracy			
Few if any False Alarms			
Scheduling Scans			
Frequency Options			
Detection and Removal Options			
Scanning Location Options			
Individual Files			
Directories			
Multiple Drives			
Network Drives			
Log Files			

REMOVAL AND RECOVERY OPTIONS

Third-party Test Results & Reviews

Consistent Leader in Detection & Removal of Malware

Quarantine Area

Automatic Disinfection

Ask Before Action Taken

Save Copy of Infected File Before Disinfection

Success in Removing Viruses

Number of File Fragments After Disinfection

SUPPORT

Help System Available

Quality of Documentation

Malware Encyclopedia

Quality of Descriptions

(Continued)

TABLE 6.11 Antivirus Software Evaluation Form (*Continued*)

Features to Consider	Antivirus Program A	Antivirus Program B	Antivirus Program C
Detail Provided			
Comprehensive			
Total Number of Malware Databased			
Types of Malware Documented			
Technical Support			
Quality of Service			
Professional			
Friendly & Helpful			
Experienced & Knowledgeable			
Efficient			
Follow Up			
Hours of Operation			

Availability/Hold Time

Average Response Time

Methods (phone, e-mail, mail, Internet)

Customer Training

On- and Off-site Options

Available Consulting Services

OVERALL SCORE

being the best score. For a quick evaluation, browse over items listed in a category such as "Cost" and assign a value to the entire category (instead of ranking each individual item). Weight scores to determine what categories or features matter the most in the evaluation.

Another option is to simply use a checkmark, plus, or minus symbol to quickly outline features supported by various antivirus programs. When done reviewing each package, analyze the form and rank or weight features according to a list of predetermined priorities and needs.

Installation and Setup

Thanks to some standardization of setup programs and methods over the last few years, users may simply follow directions on a screen, using default values if desired, to install and configure commercial antivirus software. Online scanners, such as HouseCall and McAfee VirusScan, are even easier to use, not requiring any local setup—it's all done through an Internet browser!

General Installation Procedures

The concept and basic procedure for installing commercial software on a Macintosh is basically the same as installing on a Windows-based machine. Installations of antivirus packages, not dependent upon the operating system, support different options and setup screens. Use the General Installation Procedures below to install antivirus software.

- Read the installation instructions provided with commercial software to review system requirements, known compatibility issues, and other installation instructions.

- Back up work before initiating the install.

- Validate that you have a boot disk and emergency disk on hand before installing software.

- Disable any existing antivirus software before running the setup/install program.

- Exit (Quit) all open programs.

- Run the setup/install program and follow the directions on the screen, using default values if desired.

- Reboot the machine after installation and test functionality of all software. Enable software previously disabled, if desired.

- Register software following installation, saving a copy of registration information on paper for your files.

- Create new boot, emergency, and antivirus disks during or after installation of antivirus software.

- Update virus strings database files immediately following successful installation of antivirus software.

- Scan an EICAR test file with the newly installed antivirus program. If it is *not* detected, double-check the test and troubleshoot to identify the problem.

- Confirm configuration options of newly installed software by accessing the program through the taskbar or Programs group in the Start menu. Run a scan on all drives.

- If something doesn't work after installation, such as not being able to receive e-mail, validate antivirus software configurations or disable them completely until the problem can be identified.

Following successful installation, configure the entire workstation for optimal performance. If a variety of other programs are configured to run in memory on the system, consider disabling a few to enable an antivirus on-access scanner.

If more than one antivirus package resides on a system only configure one to run in memory, as an on-access scanner. Running two on-access scanners is not recommended since conflicts may arise. However, still keep the second program to use as an on-demand scanner and backup option to the primary package. This is very important, since no single antivirus program detects and removes all viruses in existence today.

As a general rule, install only one package at a time, testing carefully before installing an additional package. If multiple installs are all done at the same time, it makes troubleshooting of conflicts and errors more complex and difficult.

Quick-fix programs offered as shareware or freeware may not be as easy to install, use, or uninstall. That's not to say that some quick-fix programs aren't better than some commercial programs—just that, in general, quick-fix programs are not always as comprehensive as commercial programs. Only download quick-fix programs from reputable sites and use carefully, at your own risk.

Installing F-Prot for PC

F-Prot is free to home users, is very robust, is a quick Internet download (small file size), compatible with many PC operating systems, and fits on a floppy for removal of system-based viruses. Follow the instructions below to obtain and install F-Prot on a PC computer.

1. Download F-Prot from Frisk at http://www.complex.is/, along with the Sign.def and Macro.def files. After clicking on a link to download each of the packages a window like the one in Figure 6.1 will appear. Save files to the Desktop for easy file management and wait for the download to be completed.

2. Unzip all files into a new folder called F-Prot. If using an unzip utility such as WinZip, right-click and drag files to a new location on the Desktop and let go to access pop-up menu options for extracting the file to the Desktop or to a folder. You may use

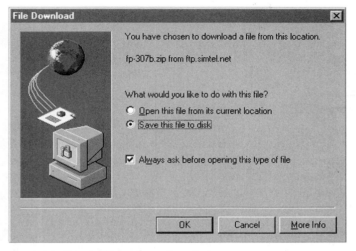

Figure 6.1   Downloading software from the Internet.

this same method to drag and extract Sign.def and Macro.def into the F-Prot folder. If existing files are in the destination folder with the same name, which is usually the case during this installation, overwrite them with the newly downloaded Sign.def and Macro.def files, as shown in Figure 6.2.

3. Review the contents of the newly installed F-Prot folder and run additional setup programs, if available and desired. Create an EICAR test file and then run F-Prot.exe to test basic functionality.

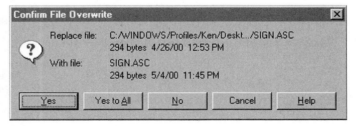

Figure 6.2   Confirm overwrites of old files with newly downloaded virus signature files.

See the segment on fitting F-Prot on a floppy disk, featured later in this section, to create a disk with F-Prot antivirus software. If malware does infect the computer, F-Prot on a disk may be used to remove malware after the system is booted from a clean boot disk.

Installing Achilles'Shield for PC

Achilles'Shield, made by InDefense, is an excellent complement to traditional commercial antivirus programs. Achilles'Shield is a proactive program, working to prevent the infection of malware by monitoring activity rather than by virus strings database comparisons. Because this program does not use a virus strings database, constant updates are not required.

Achilles'Shield has been tested for compatibility with Norton Antivirus 5.0, PC-cillin 6.0, InoculateIT 5.0, and McAfee VirusScan 4.0 at the time of writing this book. Follow the instructions below to obtain and install Achilles'Shield on a PC computer.

1. Format a floppy disk if you intend to create a rescue disk during the installation of Achilles'Shield (strongly recommended).

2. Download Achilles'Shield from InDefense at http://www.indefense.com/. After saving the file to the hard drive run the achilles.exe self-extracting ZIP file, as shown in Figure 6.3.

3. Navigate to the Achilles folder on the C drive, or custom location chosen during the unzipping process, and run SETUP.EXE. Follow instructions on the introductory setup and licensing screens and then choose a destination folder for Achilles'Shield.

4. After choosing the Programs group the installation of Achilles'Shield begins, as shown in Figure 6.4.

5. Once the first part of the installation is complete the rescue disk is created. I strongly recommend creating a rescue disk during the installation. Label the rescue disk and store it in a safe place when done.

WinZip Self-Extractor - achilles.exe ☒

To unzip all files in achilles.exe to the specified
folder press the Unzip button.

Unzip to folder:

| \achilles | Browse... |

☑ Overwrite files without prompting

Unzip

Run WinZip

Close

About

Help

Unzipping data1.cab

Figure 6.3   Run self-extracting ZIP file to extract Achilles'Shield setup files.

6. The last major part of the installation involves an
   inoculation routine, where Achilles'Shield profiles
   the system and inoculates the system against malware. Figure 6.5 shows the screen that begins the
   inoculation process.

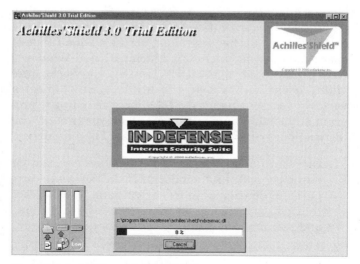

Figure 6.4   Installation of Achilles'Shield.

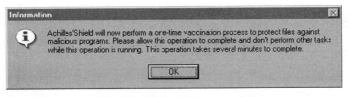

Figure 6.5   Achilles'Shield inoculation during an install.

7. Restart the computer when the installation is complete.

8. Run Achilles'Shield Task Manager from the Achilles'Shield folder in the Programs group (or customized location) to access program options and schedule events. For example, click on All Local Drives—All tools and select Edit Task... from the Task menu to configure scanning and scheduling options. Figure 6.6 shows the scheduling option for the All Local Drives—All tools task.

Installing Norton Antivirus for PC

Norton Antivirus (NAV), by Symantec Corporation, is a leading antivirus solution for both home and corporate users. NAV solutions are robust across a wide range of operating systems, including Macintosh and Windows. NAV is now integrated with Norton SystemWorks, providing users with a complete utility suite to meet a variety of computing needs. NAV is an easy-to-use program supporting a wide range of features. Follow the instructions below to install NAV on a PC computer.

1. Download NAV from http://www.symantec.com/ or purchase it from a vendor to install on your computer. If downloading from Symantec you'll notice that you are able to interrupt the large download and resume it at a later time—very nice feature.

2. After successfully downloading NAV you'll notice a new icon on the Desktop, Launch   Norton

Antivirus 2000. Running this program, or the setup program from a commercial CD ROM, initiates the setup of NAV 2000 on a computer.

3. Follow the instructions on the welcome screen and software license agreement screens to begin the installation process.

4. Add checkmarks next to desired auto-protection, weekly scheduling of scans, and startup scan options, as shown in Figure 6.7.

5. Add checkmarks next to e-mail scanning options desired and select the action for NAV to take when malware is discovered within e-mail. E-mail pro-

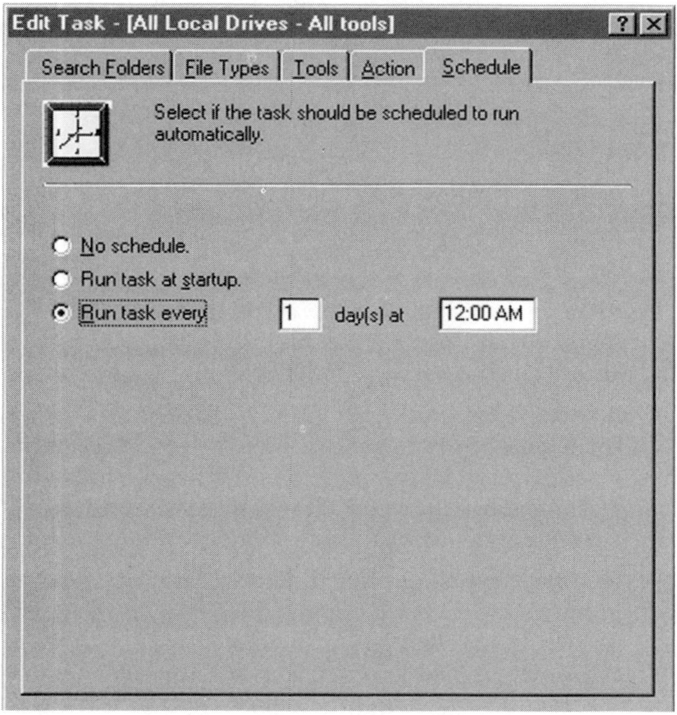

Figure 6.6   Achilles'Shield schedule options for the All Local Drives– All tools **task.**

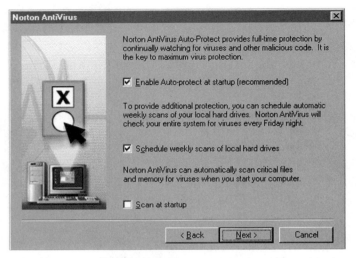

Figure 6.7 **Auto-protection, weekly scans, and startup scan options for NAV 2000 during installation.**

grams must be closed, if e-mail scanning is enabled, to allow NAV 2000 to install correctly.

6. After reviewing current settings, NAV 2000 begins copying files.

7. Although optional, it is recommended that the registration form be completed during the installation.

8. Although optional, it is highly recommended that LiveUpdate is run, rescue disks are created, and a startup scan is completed immediately following installation. Figure 6.8 shows checkbox options for configuring each of these options.

9. Restart your computer and run LiveUpdate when prompted to do so. If LiveUpdate fails for any reason, such as a bad Internet connection, feel free to cancel it out and perform it at a later time.

10. After restarting you'll also be asked to configure the NAV 2000 Netscape Plug-in Setup, as shown in Figure 6.9.

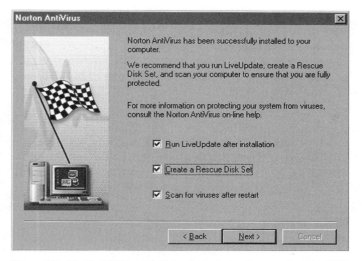

Figure 6.8 LiveUpdate, rescue disks, and startup scan options for NAV 2000 during installation.

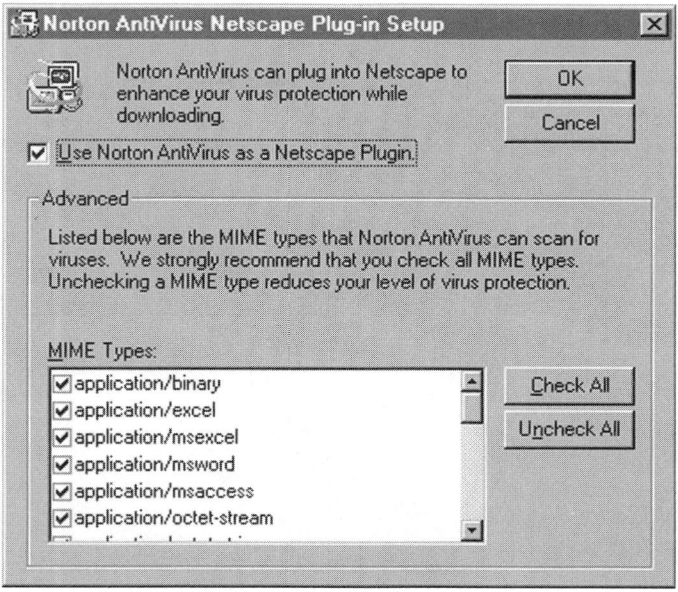

Figure 6.9   NAV 2000 Netscape Plug-in Setup.

11. If using trialware you'll notice a NAV 2000 screen upon startup that gives you options to purchase NAV, relicense, try until the trialware period expires, or get more information on the product. Click on the try option to make use of NAV during the trial period.

12. Launch NAV through the taskbar icon or Programs group under the Start menu. Click on the Options button to configure NAV 2000 options, as shown in Figure 6.10. Validate all configurations and update as desired. Create an EICAR test file and then run NAV 2000 to test basic functionality.

Creating a Boot Disk

Create a new boot disk whenever you update your operating system to avoid conflicts or errors in using a boot disk during an emergency situation. Having a clean, locked, boot disk on hand during an emergency

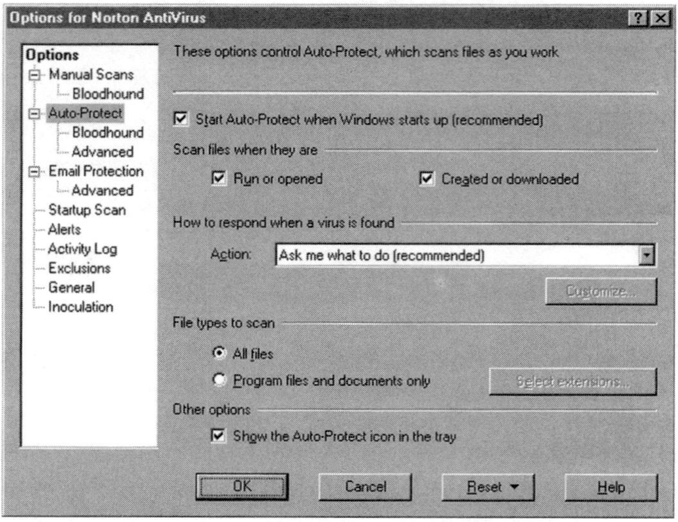

Figure 6.10   Configuring NAV 2000 options after initial setup.

situation makes a world of difference in some malware infection situations.

When creating a boot disk use a new floppy disk in good condition. The floppy disk in drive A will be completely erased, and dedicated to serving as a backup boot disk (not for normal use).

After creating a boot disk consider copying over other files that may be of assistance, as outlined in Appendix C. This is especially important if options such as accessing antivirus or other information on a CD are desired when running a computer from a boot disk. Also consider creating an emergency/rescue disk and a disk with antivirus, such as F-Prot covered later in this section.

When done creating a boot disk, lock the disk by moving the plastic tab to where a hole can be seen through the disk case. This prevents the boot disk from becoming infected by any malware. Verify that the disk works as designed by restarting the computer from the newly created boot disk in the A drive (CMOS boot order settings may need to be temporarily changed). Store the disk in a safe place, away from electronic devices and extremes of temperature.

Creation of boot disks, capable of starting up a computer, differs among various operating systems. Specific instructions are provided below for DOS, Windows, and Macintosh operating systems.

DOS. On any DOS-based machine or Windows machine using the MS-DOS prompt, enter FORMAT A: /S to create a system (boot) disk.

Windows 3.X. Open File Manager in the Main program group or use the Run... menu option of the File menu to load File Manager. Select Make System Disk... from the Disk menu and follow the instructions on the screen.

Windows 95/98/NT. Open My Computer and right-click on the A drive to select Format.... Select Format

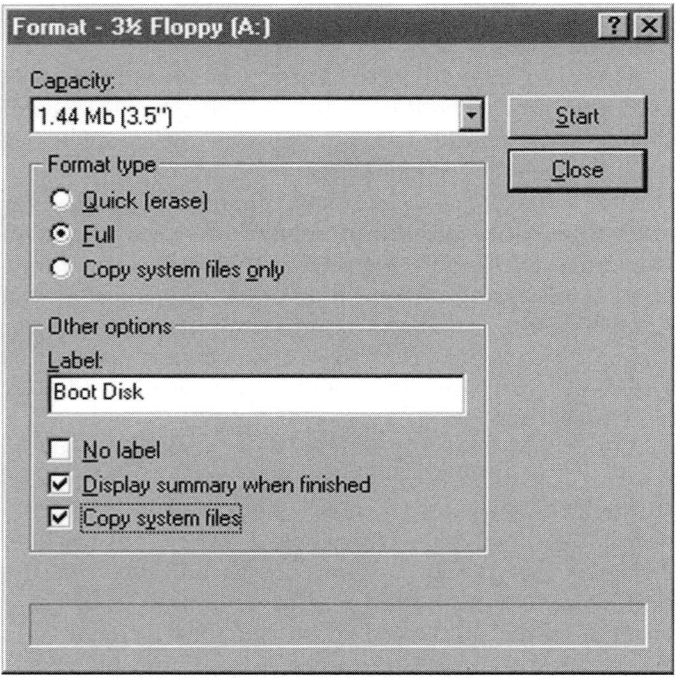

Figure 6.11 **Creating a boot disk in Windows 95/98.**

Type "Full" and place a checkmark next to Copy system files, as shown in Figure 6.11, and click on Start.

Another option in Windows 95/98 is to open the Add/Remove control panel, click on the Startup Disk tab, and click on Create Disk....

Windows NT users may use a Windows 95/98 boot disk to start up a Windows NT computer to access FAT partitions. Access to secure NTFS partitions is not allowed when booting from a floppy disk. If a computer is configured with a FAT "C" partition and NTFS "D" partition, the C drive may be scanned with antivirus software off of a floppy when booting from a Windows 95/98 boot disk.

Macintosh. Open the `System` folder and manually copy over the `System` and `Finder` files to a disk. PowerBook users and various LC users may also need to copy over system enabler files.

If these files are too large to fit on a disk, which is often the case with newer Macintosh operating systems, obtain a copy of a CD that boots the computer. If you're not sure a CD will boot the system, try booting up the Macintosh from the CD. To startup a Macintosh from a CD, hold down `shift-option-command-delete` during the boot process or the `C` key. Once the smiling Macintosh face appears you may let up on the keys.

Expert users may want to make copies of the `System` and `Finder` files to remove unnecessary resources with `ResEdit`. After editing, attempt to copy over necessary files to a newly formatted Macintosh floppy disk.

Creating Antivirus Disks

Having functional (not a setup program) antivirus software on a floppy disk or CD is very important for rescue situations. When attempting to remove viruses from a system, exclusive access may be gained by booting the system from a clean floppy disk. Ideally, antivirus software, available on floppy disk or CD, is then run from a location other than the hard drive to detect and remove viruses on the computer.

Most commercial programs have grown in file size over the years to accommodate extra code required for a graphical user interface and additional antivirus features/functionality. When considering the purchase of commercial antivirus software, look closely at this option to determine if the program is able to be run from the CD or off of a floppy disk.

Fitting F-Prot on a Floppy Disk

F-Prot is a popular choice for home users. It is free, small, compatible, robust, and fits on a floppy disk for emergency situations. Follow the steps below to fit F-Prot on a floppy disk.

1. Download and install a copy of F-Prot, and updated `Sign.def` and `Macro.def` files, as described earlier in this section.

2. Copy the following files to a disk: `F-Prot.exe`, `English.txo`, `Sign.def`, `Sign2.def`, and `nomacro.def`.

3. Rename `nomacro.def` on the floppy disk to `macro.def`.

This method enables users to use F-Prot to scan for malware other than macro viruses, which are easily removed within a Windows environment. When using F-Prot to scan for viruses in an emergency situation, make sure you reboot the computer from the hard disk and scan all files for malware using a complete version of F-Prot or other antivirus software.

Creating Emergency Disks

Use antivirus, utility, or operating system programs to create emergency disks. For example, under Windows NT users may run `RDISK.EXE` (enter into `Run...` under `Start` menu) to create an emergency repair disk with backups of essential files.

EICAR Test

The EICAR test file is a good way to verify basic functionality of recently installed or updated antivirus software. Developed by the European Institute of Computer Anti-Virus Research organization, the EICAR test file is widely supported by commercial antivirus programs. The idea is simple—create an EICAR test file on your computer and run antivirus software. If the scan detects the file the antivirus software is working as designed. If the file is not detected, the EICAR test file is not supported by the program or there is a problem with the basic functionality of the antivirus program.

The EICAR test file is a simple set of characters, as shown below, saved into a text document (.txt extension).

```
X5O!P%@AP[4P^)7CC)7}    $EICAR-STANDARD-ANTIVIRUS-
TEST-FILE!$H+H*
```

Because most on-access scanners only scan program files, the EICAR test file is normally changed from a .txt extension to a .com extension (simple renaming of a file with extensions viewable). This way on-access scanners scan the newly created .com file immediately upon creation.

While running the test look validate antivirus software functionality for detection of the EICAR test file. If available and enabled, look for the following: Local and network alert methods, including sound, and quality of the warning messages, quarantine or other action taken, and log file results.

Remember that the EICAR test file is only an indication of proper functionality. All an EICAR test really indicates it that the on-access scanner did scan the test file, detected the known EICAR string, and was able to take appropriate action (as configured by the user). Nevertheless, the EICAR test file is a risk free method to test a recently installed antivirus program. It is a much better option than obtaining and scanning actual malware, unnecessarily putting a computer at risk.

Updates and Upgrades

Updates refer to the regular updating of virus strings database files. Upgrades refer to changes made in the program itself, such as being Y2K compliant or improving functionality of a program.

It's a good idea to update often, on a regular schedule such as once a week. Updating when there is a major epidemic, such as the recent I Love You worm, is also a good idea. Staying informed about current threats In the Wild goes a long way toward prevention of malware infections.

Upgrades are normally done on a less-frequent basis. Upgrades can sometimes be expensive and may not always provide a customer with significant changes in functionality, interface, or ease of use. Carefully analyzing the differences between two different versions of a package helps users to discern the value of an upgrade.

New Software May Not Have Updated Files

New computer users often assume that their computer is protected by the antivirus software that came with the computer. The fact is that bundled antivirus software on new computers often contains severely outdated virus strings database files. As computers are manufactured and bundled for sale, a master image disk is often used for long periods of time (several months at a time). Even if an updated image file is used to copy software to a new computer, it still takes a certain amount of time before the computer ever enters the house of the consumer. For this reason, all antivirus software should be considered outdated, even on new computers. Table 6.12 lists several Internet locations, available at the time of writing this book, for obtaining antivirus signature file updates online.

Antivirus Solutions for Older Computers and Operating Systems

As older computers and operating systems continue to become obsolete by the fast-growing technology of today, users will find it increasingly difficult to obtain hardware, software, and support.

Some versions of DOS include Microsoft Antivirus, MSAV. Unfortunately, this antivirus solution is not very robust and is widely criticized. Several DOS-sup-

TABLE 6.12 Online Antivirus Software Update Sites

AntiVirus Toolkit Pro (AVP)	http://www.avp.com/new_updates.html ftp://ftp.avp.com/pub/update32.exe
Command Antivirus	http://www.commandcom.com/html/defupdate.html
Dr. Solomon Antivirus	http://www.nai.com/asp_set/download/dats/dr_solomon_4x.asp
F-Prot	http://www.complex.is/f-prot/Download.html
InoculateIT	http://antivirus.cai.com/cgi-bin/ipe/update.cgi
McAfee Antivirus	http://www.nai.com/asp_set/download/dats/superdat.asp http://www.nai.com/asp_set/download/dats/mcafee_4x.asp
Microsoft Security Bulletins	http://www.microsoft.com/security/bulletins/
Norton Antivirus	http://www.symantec.com/avcenter/download.html
Microsoft Office Updates	http://www.officeupdate.com/
PC-cillin, Trend AntiVirus	http://www.antivirus.com/download/updates.htm
Windows 95/98	http://www.microsoft.com/downloads/
Vet Anti-virus	http://www.vet.com.au/html/update.html

ported antivirus programs are still available, some of which are even checkmark certified, as noted earlier in this section.

F-Prot is a great program for both DOS- and Windows-based operating systems, being small in size, compatible, and robust. McAfee VirusScan for DOS is another well-founded DOS-based antivirus product.

A large variety of shareware DOS antivirus programs may also be downloaded from popular sites such as About.com and CIAC. Although many shareware programs are scanners only, some do provide complete detection and malware removal functionality.

Uninstalling Antivirus Software

Removing commercial antivirus programs can sometimes be a hassle but is fairly automated on new operating systems. On PCs with a Windows operating system, open the Add/Remove control panel to select a program to uninstall, as shown in Figure 6.12. Click on the Uninstall button to begin the uninstall process.

During the uninstall, a prompt may appear asking if a shared file should be kept or removed. As a general rule, keep shared files in case they are used by a different program. Figure 6.13 shows an uninstall screen where the user is prompted to keep or remove a shared filed.

If an uninstall fails for any reason, manual uninstall methods may be taken to remove software from a computer. Some manual methods may also be required if an uninstall only partially removes software files from a drive. While manually removing files keep in mind that newer computers often have a lot of hard drive space available—and deleting files can be dangerous. Leaving a few files on the drive may be a better solution than accidentally removing essential files during a manual removal of software.

To manually remove software look for files related to the name of the program. A great starting point is the Programs folder commonly located on the C drive of PC computers. If related files are found, use the dates associated with the files to perform an advanced Find...by date. Sometimes files of an install have the same modification date and may be found with the advanced Find option. Using Find... to locate related files by name may also help to locate files of interest.

Once files have been located and tagged for possible deletion, drag them into the Recycle Bin and restart the computer. Placing a file in the Recycle Bin effectively disables it from functioning but does not remove

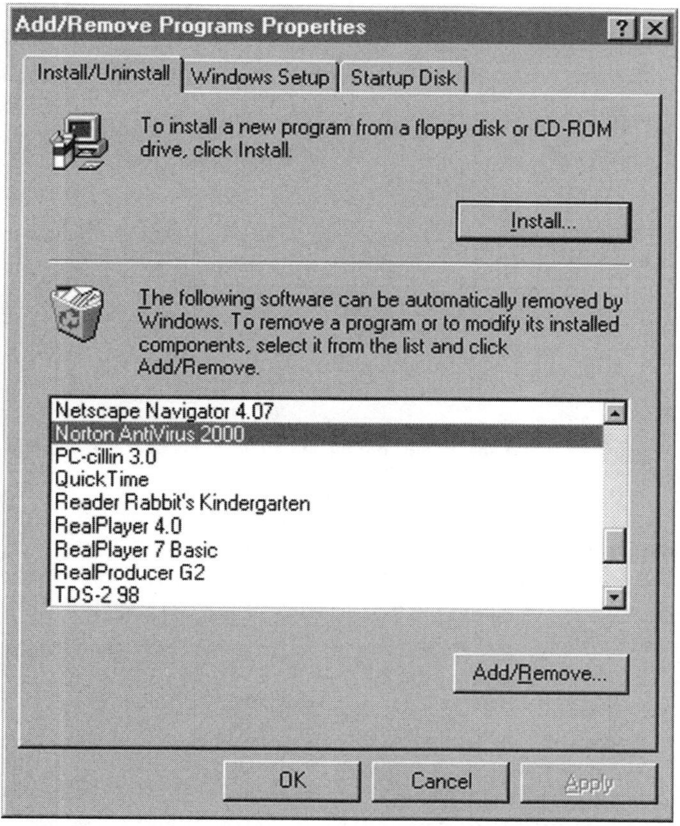

Add/Remove Programs Properties [?] [X]

Install/Uninstall | Windows Setup | Startup Disk

To install a new program from a floppy disk or CD-ROM drive, click Install.

[Install...]

The following software can be automatically removed by Windows. To remove a program or to modify its installed components, select it from the list and click Add/Remove.

Netscape Navigator 4.07
Norton AntiVirus 2000
PC-cillin 3.0
QuickTime
Reader Rabbit's Kindergarten
RealPlayer 4.0
RealPlayer 7 Basic
RealProducer G2
TDS-2 98

[Add/Remove...]

[OK] [Cancel] [Apply]

Figure 6.12 Using `Add/Remove` control panel to remove software in a Windows operating system.

it from the computer until the Recycle Bin is emptied at a later time. Test functionality of all software programs to make sure that none of the files in the Recycle Bin is required or used by other programs. If everything works just fine, feel free to put Recycle Bin files on a disk to back them up and then empty the Recycle Bin.

If software does not work correctly after placing files in the Recycle Bin, open the Recycle Bin and restore files one by one. Right-click on files that you believe

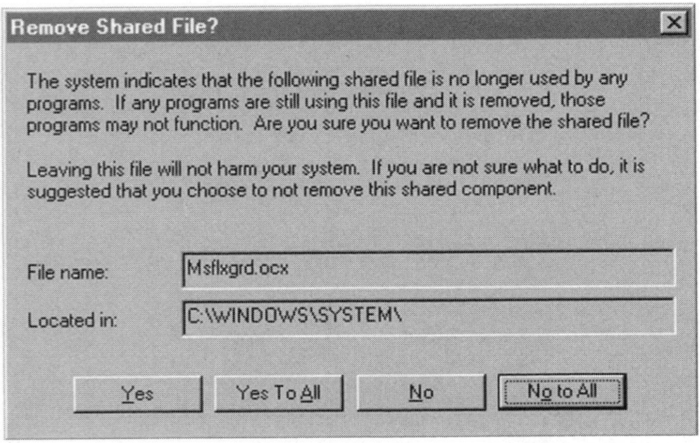

Remove Shared File?   ☒

The system indicates that the following shared file is no longer used by any programs. If any programs are still using this file and it is removed, those programs may not function. Are you sure you want to remove the shared file?

Leaving this file will not harm your system. If you are not sure what to do, it is suggested that you choose to not remove this shared component.

File name: Msflxgrd.ocx

Located in: C:\WINDOWS\SYSTEM\

[Yes]   [Yes To All]   [No]   [No to All]

Figure 6.13   Keep shared files during an uninstall to avoid removing files that another program may still use.

are needed to solve the problem and select Restore. Restart the application in question, and the computer if needed, to test functionality again. If everything works fine, continue testing all other programs on the computer. If things don't work, put the file back into the Recycle Bin or restore additional files until troubleshooting is completed.

On a Macintosh the process is similar, searching out program files and the System folder for files in question, moving files to the Trash until all software work as desired. Macintosh users often need to remove both control panel(s) and extension(s)—check each system folder carefully for related files.

If you've tried automated uninstall and manual methods for removing software with no success try contacting the antivirus software company for additional help. If you have Internet access, look for uninstall help on Internet Web sites. Companies often have detailed instructions on how to troubleshoot and uninstall software from a machine.

Removing Malware

Once an infection has occurred the best option for most users, most of the time, is to use commercial antivirus solutions to remove malware from an infected system.

Why Some Malware Can't Be Removed Easily

Encryption Issues

Removing viruses such as Monkey and One Half, which encrypt data, may effectively erase the contents of a drive when the virus is removed from the system. In the case of One Half, it encrypts the last two unencrypted cylinders on a hard disk each time an infected computer is booted. As long as One Half is resident on the system it decrypts information when requested so that the infection and encryption of data remain hidden to the user. When One Half is removed from the computer, the decryption of encrypted data on the hard drive is also removed.

Malware-Controlled System

Malware running in memory, in an effort to avoid detection and removal and spread on an infected drive, may partially control a system. Using the cardinal rule for disinfection, explained later in this section, a user may bypass malware that normally boots into memory when a system is started up. Once the malware is no longer running in memory, antivirus programs may be used to disinfect a system.

Antivirus Program Weakness

Antivirus programs are not able to detect and remove all malware. There are even situations where an antivirus program is able to detect but not remove malware from a system. If this occurs, follow the cardinal rule of disinfection below with several different antivirus programs and methods to remove malware from the system.

Multiple Infections

Backing up files prior to disinfection is always important, especially when more than one virus is detected on a system. Multiple infections on a drive may complicate the removal procedure and compromise file disinfection and rescue attempts. Sometimes using more than one program or method may help with disinfection and rescue efforts. Unfortunately, multiple infections, such as two Master Boot Record (MBR) infections, can be very complicated and difficult to execute successfully.

The normal booting process of a computer involves loading MBR information off of a hard disk as shown in Figure 7.1.

When an MBR virus infects a disk, it overwrites the MBR with virus code and stores a copy of the original MBR on the hard disk. When the virus code is executed during startup it references MBR information on the hard disk to start up the computer as shown in Figure 7.2. This helps to conceal the presence of the MBR infection while loading the virus into memory during the startup process.

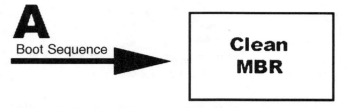

Figure 7.1 Clean booting process involving the Master Boot Record.

When an antivirus program detects an MBR virus it may attempt to overwrite the virus code in the MBR with the clean MBR copy on the hard disk. When only one MBR virus is present on a system this effectively removes the MBR virus from the MBR and restores the computer to normal MBR settings.

When a second MBR virus infects the already infected MBR it uses the same method as the first MBR virus to infect the drive. The new MBR virus code overwrites the MBR and stores a copy of the existing MBR code (which is virus code from the first virus) to the hard disk. The hard disk copy of the MBR is stored in the same exact location as the first virus, shown in Figure 7.2. The end result is that the original clean MBR is overwritten with virus code from the first virus when the second virus stores the existing MBR code to the hard drive, as shown in Figure 7.3.

Notice in Figure 7.3 that there is no MBR information, only virus code information. The computer will not be able to boot following a second MBR infection. When antivirus software attempts to remove the MBR virus, it uses the same method as previously described,

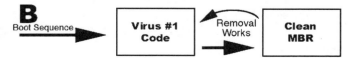

Figure 7.2 Boot process after a single Master Boot Record virus infection.

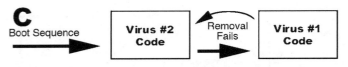

Figure 7.3   Boot process after two MBR virus infections.

overwriting the MBR with information from the MBR data stored on the hard disk. This effectively removes the second MBR virus to infect the computer but places virus code from the first virus back into the MBR. If attempts are then made to remove this virus from the MBR, there is no MBR reference on the hard disk to successfully restore the MBR. The MBR needs to be rebuilt with a program such as F-DISK (recommended for experts only).

Generic Detection

Some viruses are detected by antivirus software as generic or inexact. When inexact detection occurs a generic repair may corrupt or damage an infected file. Using a second antivirus program to detect and remove malware may help to better identify and successfully remove malware from a computer.

Online resources are another tool that can be used to learn more about an individual virus. Use several online databases to search for all possible names, keywords, and phrases related to the virus. Take the time to learn how each database works, making use of common search tools such as placing phrases inside of quotes, using "+" to include words in a search, or "2" to exclude words from a search. Some resources, such as VGrep at http://www.virusbtn.com/VGrep/, offer cross-reference searches.

Misdiagnosis

Antivirus programs may also misdiagnose a virus found on a machine. If a misdiagnosed virus is removed from infected files, corruption or damage may occur. Having good backups on file, made on a regular basis, helps to rescue information that may be damaged or corrupted by malware or removal of malware from a system.

Inadequate Removal

Some viruses are like the Energizer Bunny, they just keep coming back, coming back, and coming back! Reinfection often occurs when all media are not disinfected once an infection is detected on a machine. Sometimes users will scan all regular files but forget about e-mail files. After opening up old e-mails and related attachments, reinfection may occur on a system.

Many users take actions to remove malware from an infected computer but fail to scan all floppy disks and other media. As infected floppy disks and files are reintroduced to the system, they may reinfect the computer. This is even more likely when a user has failed to install an on-access scanner and engages in continued high-risk behaviors.

Another reason for reinfection stems from files that are traditionally more difficult or unlikely to be scanned by antivirus software. Some types of compressed files, or files with passwords or security encryption, may not be able to be scanned as well as normal files on a system. If a virus is missed in a scan of a compressed or nonstandard infected file, the system may be reinfected when the file is opened at a later date.

Viruses running in memory may also reinfect a drive after files are cleaned by antivirus software. Use the Cardinal Rule of Disinfection, below, to avoid this scenario.

Continued High-Risk Behavior

It's shocking to know that a large number of users don't even use antivirus software or update it on a regular basis. Many open every attachment like it's a winning ticket to a state lottery, not even thinking twice about the risk of malware infection. Hopefully, after massive outbreaks from malware such as Melissa and Love Letter, users will take the initiative to get educated and take proactive actions against malware.

Skeletal Remains

Fragments of viruses are sometimes left behind by an antivirus program following disinfection. Such fragments are sometimes enough to make an antivirus program detect the fragment as a virus—even if it is a nonfunctional fragment of a virus. When using two or more on-demand scanners, they may sometimes have conflicting reports because of skeletal remains and differences between the two packages regarding detection and removal of viruses from a system.

Removing Malware from an Infected System

Formatting the Hard Disk Is
Never Required

Reformatting a hard disk is never required to remove malware from a system. Ironically, it is possible for a user to erase the contents of a drive and still have an infection in the MBR! Nothing is more frustrating than to erase the contents of a drive only to find that a malware is still present on the system. Follow the instructions in this section to gain exclusive control over an infected system before attempting to remove malware with antivirus programs.

Back Up Data Before Disinfecting

Back up files before attempting to remove malware from a file. Sometimes the removal of malware from a file leaves it in a corrupt or unusable state. If a backup copy of the file is on hand, even if it is infected, alternative disinfection methods or programs may be used in an attempt to rescue data.

Some antivirus programs provide users with the option to create a copy of a file before attempting to disinfect. Another great option for backing up infected files is to use a quarantine area. Supported by several antivirus programs, quarantine areas enable users to safely store questionable files in a secure area and back them up before attempting to disinfect.

Cardinal Rule of Disinfection

The cardinal rule of malware removal is to boot from a clean, locked, boot disk before running antivirus from a location other than an infected hard drive (e.g., floppy disk, CD). This provides exclusive access to a drive that may otherwise be controlled by a malware infection.

Do a cold boot, where your computer is turned off for at least 10 seconds, before you turn it on. This gives the hard drive enough time to stop spinning and will remove all programs running in resident memory. Put your boot disk into drive A and start up your computer.

After you boot the computer from your clean, locked, boot disk, eject the disk and put in a clean, locked, antivirus disk and run antivirus software from the A drive. Using locked disks prevents emergency disks from becoming infected or being compromised in any way by malware. Do not run antivirus software from the hard drive unless no other option is available.

Once the hard drive is disinfected, reboot the system from the hard drive and run antivirus software from the hard drive to scan the entire computer. Following a hard drive scan, scan *all* other media, especially floppy disks, to avoid reinfecting the system.

Exceptions to the Cardinal Rule

Gaining exclusive control of a system before using an antivirus program to remove malware from a computer is not always required. For example, the macro viruses are easily removed from an infected system, not requiring a boot from a clean floppy disk.

As a general rule of thumb, use antivirus software to scan and remove malware from a system before taking the more time-consuming steps to reboot from a clean floppy disk. If malware is detected during a scan, take appropriate action. If malware is not able to be removed, follow the cardinal rule above to remove malware from the system. Even if malware is removed without the cardinal rule system, it's a good idea to boot from a clean floppy disk to ensure that no malware exists on a system.

Another issue may be the robustness of the antivirus program currently being used on a system to detect and remove malware from a system. If a program is not very robust or uses badly outdated virus strings database files, it may not detect and remove viruses in any situation—even if exclusive control over a system is gained prior to a scan. Using two on-demand scanners with updated virus strings database files, on a regular basis, is a rock solid method that I strongly recommend to serious computer users.

Using Antivirus Software to Scan and Remove Malware

Verify configurations for on-demand and on-access scanning options immediately after installing a new antivirus program. Pay especially close attention to details such as scanning program files only or all files, heuristic scan options, and actions to take when malware is detected on a computer.

To access scanning options for on-access antivirus programs double-click on the taskbar icon for the program and select the options of choice. On-demand scanners may also be available through this method as well as launching them from a desktop icon or Programs group option under the Start menu.

Configure antivirus programs to run a single on-access scanner at all times. Run the on-demand scanner on occasion, or when new files or media are brought into a system. Run a second on-demand scanner periodically to back up the primary antivirus package on a computer. If available, schedule regular scans for when a computer is not in use to scan the computer on a regular basis. If computers are networked, work with system operators to run remote scans and implement network security and antivirus protection solutions.

Scanning Attachments and Individual Files

If an on-access scanner is enabled, users are reasonably protected while they work. As files are opened, including attachments, they are scanned for malware. To be on the safe side I regularly recommend scanning attachments with an on-demand scanner before accessing a new file or disk.

To scan an attachment use the File menu to save attachments of interest to the hard drive. Navigate to the saved attachments and then right-click to see if antivirus scanning options appear on the pop-up menu. If they do, select the antivirus menu of choice to run a scan on the file. The other method is to open up the on-demand scanner from the Programs group in the Start menu and then point the program to the individual files or folders to be scanned.

Reports

A report is normally kept by antivirus software to record events surrounding detection and removal of malware from a computer. Reviewing such reports may help to identify patterns of risk behavior, when a computer is infected, the types of malware detected on a computer, and what files were infected by malware. Review reports in antivirus programs before there is an infection so that they are easily understood and helpful during malware infections (if any do occur at a later date).

Using a PC Boot Disk

Perform a cold boot, where your computer is turned off for at least 10 seconds before you turn it on. Put a boot disk into drive A and start up the computer. Change the CMOS setup to boot from the A disk first, if necessary, and boot from the floppy disk.

To change the CMOS startup sequence press the appropriate key, as shown on the screen, to access the CMOS setup. F2 and Delete are two common options for entering the CMOS setup during the first part of a system startup. Use arrow keys, Enter, and Escape to navigate through CMOS screens until the boot order can be set to start from a floppy disk first. If changes are made, save changes and reboot the system.

After successfully booting the system from a boot disk the A: prompt should appear as A:\> on the screen. Enter DOS commands to run antivirus software from the A drive or CD-ROM.

If antivirus software is available on floppy disk, such as F-Prot, simply eject the boot disk and insert the F-Prot antivirus disk. Then type DIR to see a directory list of files on the floppy disk. Look for files with .exe or .com extensions. In the case of F-Prot you simply type F-PROT to run the F-PROT.EXE program. After the antivirus program is launched, configure scan options and initiate a scan for all files on the local hard drive.

If antivirus software is available on CD-ROM, use DOS to navigate to the CD-ROM by using commands like E: to load the E CD-ROM drive on a computer. The letter used depends upon local drive assignments for the CD-ROM drive. Then type DIR to see a directory list of files on the CD-ROM. Use CD DirectoryName, where DirectoryName is the name of a folder on the CD-ROM, and CD.. to go in and out of directories within DOS. Look for files with .exe or .com extensions. After locating the antivirus program, enter the name and configure scan options to initiate a scan for all files on the local hard drive.

After successfully removing viruses from the machine remove the disk from drive A and restart the computer. If necessary, reconfigure CMOS boot sequence settings to boot from the hard disk first (C drive in most cases) to avoid boot sector infections. After saving CMOS settings reboot the machine from the hard disk and run an antivirus scan on all media.

See Appendix C for additional DOS commands and support.

Using a Macintosh Boot Disk

Booting a Macintosh computer from a boot disk or CD-ROM is a much easier process than on a PC. Perform a cold boot, where your computer is turned off for at least 10 seconds before you turn it on. Put a boot disk into drive A and start up the computer. If using a CD-ROM, hold down the C key during the boot process to force the computer to start up from the CD-ROM operating system. If this fails for any reason, reference the CD-ROM booklet for more information on how to boot the system from the CD.

After booting from a floppy disk or CD, Macintosh users are able to enjoy a standard Macintosh operating system environment. Even though some features may be temporarily disabled, users may access files on a Macintosh computer using normal navigation strategies. This makes it easy for users to run antivirus and other utility programs to disinfect an infected hard drive.

When using two floppy disks on a computer with a single floppy drive, some swapping of disks may be required. If the operating system needs to load additional instructions from the boot disk it may ask the user to reinsert the disk. Once additional information is loaded the antivirus disk may need to be reinserted for the same reason. Although it is tempting to just run antivirus software from the hard drive, after booting from a clean floppy disk, this is not optimal—software on the hard disk may be infected. Fortunately newer machines are able to cache more information and often run from a CD instead of a floppy, resulting in few occurrences of disk swapping today.

F-DISK

As already mentioned in this section, F-DISK is a powerful tool that may help users to remove MBR-infecting viruses. This powerful program should only be used by experts to avoid catastrophic consequences.

SYS C: Overwrite

The DOS boot record may be overwritten by expert users by using the SYS C: at the DOS prompt. This may help remove various boot sector infecting viruses.

Master/Slave Swap

If more than one physical drive resides on a computer, one may be configured as the master drive (boot drive) with the other as the slave drive. If the master drive does become infected with a virus that cannot be removed easily, try using the cardinal rule of disinfection mentioned earlier in this section. If the cardinal rule for disinfection fails, consider swapping out the master drive to configure it as a slave on a different machine to remove viruses from the disk. This method is only for expert users.

To swap out a master drive, back up files and then physically remove the infected master drive from inside the computer. Then open up an uninfected computer and remove the slave drive. Reconfigure the infected master drive to be a slave, by configuring jumpers as required, and attach to the clean system. Change CMOS settings as required to recognize the drive and boot the computer from the clean master drive. Run antivirus software and remove all viruses from the system and then shut down the computer.

Remove the slave drive, reconfigure as a master, and reset both computers to their original configurations.

Then run antivirus software off of the originally infected master disk to remove all viruses from the infected slave drive. Complete the process by scanning all media, including floppy disks, to lower the risk of reinfection.

Repair of Damaged or Lost Files

Some viruses corrupt information in a random fashion, making it impossible for antivirus programs to accurately identify all files corrupted by the virus. Others may be generically identified and sloppily removed from an infected file. Some files are overwritten by a virus with garbage and must be replaced with a backup file. Others are still present on a drive but may be encrypted by a virus.

Having good backups on file is the key to successful recovery. There are no guarantees after a virus infects a drive. If good backups are in place, replacements for lost or damaged files can be done in a matter of minutes.

If backups are not on file, make some immediately. Even if a virus is on a system, and files are known to be infected, back them up! If antivirus software or other methods are used to disinfect a file and don't work, the backup copy is available for additional rescue attempts. Make sure that once a successful rescue method is identified, that all media are scanned for viruses to lower the risk of reinfecting the system.

Saving an infected Microsoft Word document can be done in several ways. Try removing the virus from the file using several different antivirus programs. If that doesn't work, try opening up the file in Microsoft Word and saving the content in other file formats, such as ASCII text, HTML, Rich Text, or image files for graphics. If this fails for some reason, try opening programs such as NotePad or WordPad and then opening the infected file. View all file types to see if data can be retrieved and temporarily saved in a new format. After removing malware from the system, import files and reformat as required.

Rescue Utilities

A variety of very helpful rescue utilities are available for all types of operating systems. Several notable programs include Norton Utilities by Symantec at http://www.symantec.com/, McAfee Utilities at http://www.mcafee.com/, Easy Recovery by Ontrack at http://www.ontrack.com/, and DataRescue at http://www.datarescue.com/.

Change Passwords if Compromised

If a system is infected with malware passwords and other sensitive information may have been compromised. This is especially true with password-stealing Trojans. As a matter of good measure, change passwords often—especially after a malware infection. This may help to lower the risk of Remote Access Tool attacks sometimes utilized by hackers to remotely gain illegal access to a computer.

Glossary

ActiveX controls   Powerful programs used to increase interactivity and functionality on Internet Web pages.

alias   Alternate or assumed name.

Also Known As (AKA)   Viruses fall under a host of names since there is no standardized method for naming viruses in the industry.

antivirus (AV)   Measures taken to defend against viruses and other related malware.

American Standard Code for Information Interchange (ASCII)   A universal method used to code characters available on a computer keyboard. For example, the letter "A" in ASCII has a value of 65. Hold down the ALT key and enter various numbers to see what the ASCII value is within a word processor.

armoured virus   A virus that is written to avoid detection and disassembly analysis.

back door   Software programmers sometimes include backdoors to circumvent passwords or other security.

Basic Input Output System (BIOS)   Instructions and setup for how a system operates. An essential part of the boot-up process on a computer. Some BIOS/CMOS settings include virus scanning features that sometimes result in software installation issues.

bit   The smallest measure of data on a computer, either a 0 or a 1. 8 bits, such as 10010110, make up a byte.

boot   When a computer is turned on and started up.

boot disk   A special disk containing startup files, capable of starting up a computer. Boot disks are an important resource to have on file in case of emergency or infection of malware.

boot sector   First logical sector of a disk.

Boot Sector Infector (BSI)   A virus that infects the boot sector of a disk. Boot sector infections occur when an attempt is made to boot the computer from an infected floppy disk.

bug   An unexpected error in a software program.

byte   A measure of data containing 8 bits. A kilobyte contains 1024 bytes. A megabyte contains 1024 kilobytes. A gigabyte contains 1024 megabytes.

cache   A small area of temporary memory located on a motherboard in a strategic location to greatly improve processing speed.

cavity virus   A virus that attempts to infect a file without increasing the length of the file, overwriting select portions of code in the host file while attempting to preserve functionality.

cold boot   When a computer is not on prior to booting. When attempting to remove viruses, a cold boot is recommended to avoid problems with viruses that may be running in memory.

companion virus   A virus that creates a companion file to run a virus program and the original program.

Computer Anti-Virus Research Organization (CARO)   An elite group of antivirus researchers, many of whom represent antivirus vendors, that exchange viruses for research purposes.

Computer Metal Oxide Semiconductor (CMOS)   A type of RAM memory used to store important configuration settings. When an internal battery is replaced on a computer, CMOS settings for items such as the date and time may need to be reset.

Disk Operating System (DOS)   Microsoft's first operating system for PC computers.

dropper A file that drops malware on a computer when run.

Easter Egg Hidden signatures sometimes added to software by a programmer.

emergency disk A disk used for emergency situations. Normally refers to an emergency disk that contains important files, such as a backup of the registry. May also reference boot disks, used to boot a system in an emergency situation.

encryption The conversion of data from one format to another. Encryption may be used to secure a document or compress data.

European Institute of Computer Anti-Virus Research (EICAR) An antivirus organization responsible for the development of the EICAR test file, used to test functionality of antivirus software.

Execute To open or run a set of commands contained within a program or script file.

false alarm An incorrect report of a virus sometimes caused by scanners that have detected viruslike activity or code on a computer. Sometimes called a false positive.

false negative When viruses go undetected by an antivirus program the result is a false negative.

false positive Commonly referred to as a false alarm. An incorrect report of a virus sometimes caused by heuristic scanners that have detected viruslike activity or code on a computer.

fast infector A virus that attempts to spread quickly throughout a system.

File Allocation Table (FAT) An index used by a computer to control files on a disk. A native DOS file system.

germ The first generation of a virus. Also called "Garden of Eden Mechanism" or "Generation One Virus."

goat file A program used by an antivirus researcher to capture and disassemble malware after a malware infection. Goat files are much less cluttered and easier to disassemble.

hacker   An individual who attempts to compromise security or illegally author or distribute malware.

heuristics   Rule-of-thumb methods used by antivirus software to detect new and undiscovered viruses based upon "viruslike" qualities.

hoax   A false report, most often seen in the form of e-mail, warning of something such as a malware infection or new virus.

HyperText Markup Language (HTML)   A foundational language used to create Internet web pages.

In the Wild (ItW)   Viruses that appear on the WildList, considered to be a threat in the field.

integrity   Correct processing and information on a computer. Integrity software compares known information on a computer with new information to identify possible compromises of integrity.

Java   A language developed by Sun Systems to author interactive cross-platform applications within files called "applets."

JavaScript   A language developed by Netscape to increase interactivity and control on Internet web pages.

logic bomb   A payload that executes once a logical argument is met, such as a specific date and time.

macro virus   A virus that infects a computer through a macro supported by software such as Microsoft Word and Excel. Macro viruses infect both Macintosh and PC operating systems.

malicious code   A set of instructions designed to execute actions of malice on a computer.

malware   Generic term that covers a wide range of unwanted software: computer viruses, denial of service attacks, droppers, Trojans, Worms and more. Putting two words together, MALicious and softWARE, renders the word malware. Sometimes referred to as rogue programs.

Master Boot Record (MBR)   The first absolute sector on a hard disk, normally containing a partition table. Floppy disks do not have a master boot record. Some viruses infect the MBR rather than the boot sector. Even if a drive is erased, the MBR is not erased, leaving a computer infected by a MBR infecting virus until the MBR is cleaned.

memory resident A program that continues to run in memory, even after termination. Also called Terminate and Stay Resident (TSR).

multipartite A virus that infects both files and boot sectors.

operating system (OS) Software used to operate a computer program, such as Windows 98 and Macintosh System 8.X.

overwrite To record new data over the top of existing data, effectively erasing original data. Some viruses overwrite data on a drive with new information, corrupting or deleting existing files on a drive.

partition A section of a disk, as identified within a partition table, often assigned values such as "C" and "D." A hard disk may contain several partitions, based upon the size of the drive and software in use.

partition table A table that is used to divide a physical hard disk into logical sections known as a partition.

payload The action that malware takes on a computer following infection. Some payloads are delayed or only activate given a unique set of logical arguments, such as the time of day and day of the month.

Personal computer (PC) A generic term that most commonly refers to computers running DOS- or Windows-based operating systems, as compared to Macintosh operating system computers.

polymorphic A virus that creates modified copies of itself when it spreads.

random access memory (RAM) Short-term memory used by a computer to run programs temporarily.

read-only memory (ROM) Memory that can only be read.

retrovirus Sometimes called an "Anti-antivirus Virus," this type of virus attacks, disables, or avoids infecting specific antivirus packages to avoid detection on an infected computer.

script   A set of computing instructions contained within a file or program. Some viruses drop a malware script in the startup directory of a computer, executing upon restart.

signature   A unique pattern of bytes within code that identifies specific malware—digital fingerprint of malware.

slow infector   A virus that spreads through a system slowly. Also called a sparse infector.

stealth   An attempt to remain concealed, using one or more techniques to avoid detection on a computer system.

Terminate and Stay Resident (TSR)   A program that remains in memory after termination. TSR viruses work to spread throughout a computer by terminating after activation and running in memory.

Trojan horse   Malicious software that masquerades as a legitimate program.

tunneling   A virus that calls original interrupt handlers in DOS and BIOS directly, bypassing monitoring programs that may be running to detect virus activity.

variant   A modified version of a virus.

virus   A program that is designed to replicate, spreading from computer to computer via host programs, sometimes carrying out malicious action (payload). There are many types of viruses with various characteristics for avoiding detection, replicating, and carrying out a payload on a computer.

vulnerability   Security compromise identified within a given program, leaving it open to malware or hacker attacks.

warm boot   A boot that takes place when a computer is already running.

worm   A program that spreads much like a virus but does not require a host program.

zip   A compressed file.

zoo   Viruses used in a controlled laboratory for testing purposes.

Troubleshooting Scenarios

Selected troubleshooting scenarios are outlined below to assist in antivirus efforts. As a general rule, scan with updated antivirus software, using the cardinal rule of disinfection, to reasonably rule out viruses during the troubleshooting process.

How do I know if I'm protected against a specific virus?

Explore your current antivirus software to see if a listing of detected viruses is available. Online vendor information may also have a list of viruses detected with various versions of their antivirus software. Update files may also include helpful information.

Run an EICAR test file to ensure basic functionality of antivirus software. Review configurations to ensure that at least one on-access scanner is working at all times and that on-demand scans are set to best meet individual needs.

The fonts on my display are all messed up—do I have a virus?

Issues surrounding fonts are normally the result of missing or corrupt fonts on a system. For example, I once used a HyperCard stack on a different computer when presenting at a regional conference. The computer at the conference did not have fonts installed that my HyperCard stack required, so the system substituted the font. This resulted in a poor display, different from the original design environment. I solved the problem by using `ResEdit` to insert `FONT` resources into the HyperCard stack resource fork.

Some viruses do have visual payloads and may adversely affect the view of a normal operating environment.

I keep getting General Protection Fault Errors.

General Protection Fault (GPF) errors are common in a Windows environment, rarely having anything to do with a virus infection on a system. It is possible that the effects of a virus upon an infected system results in a GPF, but it is more likely that software configurations and use are more likely the cause of a GPF.

I was surfing the Web and my computer bombed— do I have a virus?

Computer crashes are more frequent than anyone would like to admit. If a crash occurs at a specific point in time, such as when the browser is directed to visit a specific Internet location, there may be denial of service attacks taking place from the site in question. For example, malformed links or JavaScript exploits could be used to force a computer to crash. Although none of these examples is a virus, they do interrupt work and may result in damage to software and hardware due to unexpected crashes.

My computer is displaying a message that I'm a jerk—do I have a virus?

The Class macro virus family includes a visual payload that displays a message on a certain day of the month stating that the registered name on the computer is a jerk or other things along this same line of thought. Use updated antivirus software to detect and remove the Class virus from your computer.

When I'm surfing the Internet I get "broken pipe" errors—am I infected?

A connection problem is most likely the problem, not related to viruses. Internet connectivity involves a lot of variables, such as software and hardware setup, performance of an Internet Service Provider, routers throughout the Internet, and lines of transmission worldwide. If an error in surfing the Internet occurs, users should double-check their connection status before beginning the troubleshooting process. If errors occur on a regular basis consider fine-tuning the system with a consultant.

I see a lot of upload activity—do I have a virus?

It is normal for some uploading to occur on a daily basis, as users check e-mail and surf the Internet. However, if a significant change in uploading occurs it may be the sign of an infection. For example, I happened to notice one day that my Internet connections were slower than normal and that a large amount of data was being uploaded immediately upon connecting to the Internet. After scanning with four different antivirus programs I found that F-Prot was able to detect and remove a Trojan from my computer. The uploading activity was probably due to sensitive information being uploaded to the hacker that authored the Trojan.

Ever since I used a game my friend gave me my computer has been acting funny.

Whenever you bring a new medium into a computer it may contain a virus—even if the new medium is shrink-wrapped! Scan all new files and disks with antivirus software to lower the risk of infection. Use the cardinal rule of disinfection to rule out viruses and then troubleshoot current software configurations to restore system functionality.

I'd like to know more about a certain virus.

Search online databases for information about a given virus. Search for all forms of a name and related information to find a virus. Because malware falls under so many different names it may take a while to find malware of interest. Search more than one database and consider executing cross-searches on sites such as VGrep. See my list of online virus databases at http://antivirus.about.com/msub3.htm for more information.

Is my computer at risk as soon as I place a floppy disk into the computer?

On a PC the floppy disk is not accessed until the user attempts to view or access contents on the disk. On a Macintosh the floppy disk is automatically loaded upon insertion. If a disk contains infected files, the clean system will not become infected unless virus code is run. Although not normally recommended, users are able to copy infected files from disk to disk without causing an infection. The risk of infection comes into play with human error, such as accidentally double-clicking and opening a file instead of renaming or copying it to a new location.

My computer is taking forever to boot up—do I have a virus?

If no major changes have recently been made to a system, such as a recent installation of new software, a noticeable change in how long it takes for a computer to boot up may indicate a virus infection. A virus may be attempting to run in memory during startup or spread on the computer when the drive light is already active to avoid being detected. Scan with updated antivirus software, from a clean boot disk (cold boot), to detect and remove any malware that may be on the system.

My computer will not boot up

Multiple MBR infections may adversely affect the ability of a system to boot as designed. Perform a cold boot from a clean system disk to detect and remove any malware on the system. If an operating system is damaged or missing from a system, a boot-up error will be generated. Reinstall missing files or the operating system as required to boot the machine following disinfection of any malware that may be present on the system.

My files are garbled—do I have a virus?

Some viruses, such as Love Letter, do overwrite and corrupt files. Sometimes files are damaged by system difficulties, such as a computer crash. Many times user error is responsible for accidental changes made to various documents. Sometimes weird-looking code or formatting may appear when a file, such as a Microsoft Word file, is opened or pasted into a file of a different program.

I lost all of my files due to a virus—can I rescue them?

Using a variety of backup methods is an essential proactive measure to take to avoid such desperate situations.

If data on the drive was overwritten, such as with the One Half virus, recovery may not be very successful. Some viruses, such as Love Letter, may hide certain files. Although the files are still present on the disk, they may remain unseen and unusable to the user until the hidden attribute is disabled. Follow procedures outlined in this book to rescue files, such as saving text from an infected Word document, reinserted into Word after cleaning a system.

Use data recovery tools to rescue files deleted or lost on a disk. Having a program installed and running at all times, such as Norton Utilities, may greatly assist in data backup and recovery efforts.

After disinfection I encounter errors about a missing file.

During disinfection some files may become corrupt or deleted. Use a clean backup copy to restore functionality. If a clean backup is not on hand, attempt to rescue the file from a quarantine area, if available, or from an infected backed up file, if one was created prior to disinfection.

Look for necessary files on an install disk or CD. Other options include copying necessary files from other machines, downloading files from the Internet, or contacting local vendors.

I keep getting infected with the same virus.

Use the cardinal rule of disinfection covered in Section 7 to disinfect all media. Make a special effort to disinfect all e-mails, files in the Recycle Bin (Trash), and floppy disks. Looking up information about the virus may also help. For example, the Ethan macrovirus changes the properties of some infected Microsoft Word documents. After disinfection of the Ethan virus, the properties of previously infected files may not be updated. This may lead some users into believing that there is still an infection, when in fact all they are viewing is the harmless remnants of a previous infection.

Online Resources

Reference online resources to obtain up-to-date information about malware. Addresses included here were validated at the time of writing this book but may become invalid over time. Reference the About.com Antivirus Software site at http://antivirus.about.com/ for updated links, software downloads for Macintosh, PC, Linux, Amiga, and server solutions, read original articles, interact in chat and forum discussions, and sign up for a free weekly newsletter, *Infection Connection*.

About.com Antivirus Software

http://antivirus.about.com/

About.com Internet/Network Security

http://netsecurity.about.com/compute/netsecurity/mbody.htm

About.com Urban Legends

http://urbanlegends.about.com/

Alt.comp.virus FAQ and Mini-FAQ
http://www.sherpasoft.org.uk/acvFAQ/

Aladdin eSafe Protect
http://www.esafe.com/

Alwil Software
http://www.anet.cz/alwil/

AntiViral Toolkit Pro
http://www.avp.com/

AntiViral Toolkit Pro (AVP)
http://www.avp.com/

Comp.Virus FAQ
http://www.faqs.org/faqs/computer-virus/faq/index.html

Computer Emergency Response Team (CERT)
http://www.cert.org/

Checkware
http://chekware.simplenet.com/cmindex.htm

Command Software AntiVirus
http://www.commandcom.com/

Computer Associates
http://www.cai.com/

Computer Virus Myths
http://www.kumite.com/

Content Technologies
http://www.mimesweeper.com/

CyberSoft Vfind
http://www.cyber.com/

DataRescue
http://www.datarescue.com/

Dr. Solomon
http://www.nai.com/

ER Center (downloads & help)
http://antivirus.about.com/library/bldownld.htm

eSafe Technologies
http://www.esafe.com/

F-Secure
http://www.datafellows.com/

Frisk F-Prot
http://www.complex.is/

HackFix Organization
http://www.hackfix.org/hackfix/

Kaspersky Lab
http://www.avp.com/

Leprechaun Software
http://www.leprechaun.com.au/

McAfee/Network Associates VirusScan
http://www.nai.com/

Microsoft Corporation, Inc.
http://www.microsoft.com/

NetPro
http://www.netpro.com/

Network Associates
http://www.nai.com/

NetZ Computing Ltd
http://www.invircible.com/

NH&A
http://www.nha.com/

Norman
http://www.norman.com/

Ontrack
http://www.ontrack.com/

Panda Software
http://www.pandasoftware.com/

Reflex Magnetics
http://www.reflex-magnetics.co.uk/

Safetynet Security CafÇ
http://www.safetynet.com/

Secure Computing
http://www.westcoast.com/

SecureNet Avast
http://www.securenet.org/

Sophos
http://www.sophos.com/

Stiller
http://www.stiller.com/

Symantec
http://www.symantec.com/avcenter

Trend Micro
http://www.antivirus.com/

Virus-related FAQs
http://www.faqs.org/faqs/computer-virus/

Virus Bulletin

http://www.virusbtn.com/

Virus Research Unit—University of Tampere

http://www.uta.fi/laitokset/virus/test1999.html

Virus Test Center

http://agn-www.informatik.uni-
hamburg.de/vtc/naveng.htm

WildList Organization

http://www.wildlist.org/

DOS References

Useful DOS commands are referenced in Tables C.1 and C.2. Some commands are compatible with a wide variety of versions of DOS, while others are only available in newer versions of DOS.

TABLE C.1 Annotated DOS Commands with Examples

Command	Example	What It Does
exe *files*	. wp or wp.exe	Types the name of .exe files to execute (run) the program.
dir	dir	Directory showing files in current directory.
dir *drive*	dir a:	Directory of a different drive such as the A drive.
dir /w	dir /w	Shows files in directory in a wide listing.
dir /p	dir /p	Shows files in directory one page at a time.
dir *	dir *.*	Directory of wild match such as extensions in the example.
cd *directoryName*	cd dos	Changes directories; goes into another directory.
cd ..	cd ..	Backs out one directory; up one directory.
cd \	cd \	Changes to root directory of the current drive.
cd *path*	cd C:\DOS\	Changes directory to full path name provided.
md *name*	md games	Makes a new directory.
rd *name*	rd name	Deletes a directory as long as it contains no files.
copy *fileName*	copy notes.txt	Copies file to specified drive and path provided.
drive	a:	Example 2: copy notes.txt a:\notes\ Example 3: copy c:\DOS\label.com a:\DOSBKUO\

Command	Example	Description
copy *fileName*	copy notes.txt con	Copies a file to the console (monitor) to view it.
copy con *fileName*	copy con notes.txt *CTRL-Z to exit*	Enables you to write a file in DOS without using a word processor. Enter the command, press Enter, and enter text on a single line. Press **CTRL-Z** when done. Backup and restore when done and press Enter. Use the "copy *fileName* con" statement to view a file once it is written to the drive.
xcopy directory	drive xcopy C:\DOS a:	Copies the entire drive or directory to another.
xcopy *	xcopy * *.	Copies wildcard match such as all extensions in the example.
diskcopy a: b:	diskcopy a: b:	Copies source drive to target drive for backups.
diskcomp a: b:	diskcomp a: b:	Compares disks to verify that they are exact copies.
ren *old new*	ren hi.txt ho.txt	Renames files for existing (old) name to a new name. space, ., <, >, ^, |, *, ?, or \ more than 8 chars. Characters you don't use with file names!
del *fileName*	del notes.txt	Deletes file from the disk permanently!
del *	del *.	Deletes wild match such as all extensions in this example.
type *fileName*	type notes.txt	Types file to screen for viewing. Most useful for short files.
more *fileName*	more notes.txt	Types file to screen for viewing. Useful for lengthy files.
print *fileName*	print notes.txt	Prints the file noted.
sys *drive*	sys a:	Copies system to drive to make a boot disk.
format *drive*	format a:	Formats disk in specified drive.
format *drive*/s	format a:/s	Formats and copies system boot files to specified disk.

(Continued)

TABLE C.1 Annotated DOS Commands with Examples (Continued)

Command	Example	What It Does
date	date	Enter a new date.
time	time	Enter a new time.
ver	ver	See what version of DOS you are using.
label	label	Give your drive (disk) a name.
chkdsk	chkdsk	Check disk for memory and status.
mem	mem	Displays memory settings.
msd	msd	Accesses Microsoft Systems Diagnostics.
prompt *newPrompt*	prompt Ken	Temporarily changes DOS prompt.
help	Help	May open DOS help file.
HELP	HELP FORMAT	
COMMANDNAME	?	
?	FORMAT ?	
command ?		
dosshell	dosshell	Opens DOS Shell if available.
esc	esc	The escape key often exits programs and routines.

control-s	control-s	Stops scrolling of a directory of file. Also use Pause/Break key.
control-break	control-break	Breaks (cancels) some operations or commands.
control-c	control-c	Cancels some operations or commands.
control-alt-delete	control-alt-delete	Restarts your computer (warm boot) or loads application/tasks manager window.
cls	cls	Clears the screen.
alt-q	alt-q	Quits some programs that are running.
sys *drive*	sys c:	Formats specified drive with system files.
win	win	Opens Windows on machines with Windows installed.

TABLE C.2 Optional Files to Include on a PC Boot Disk

Boot Disk Files	Description
attrib.exe	Use this program to make files read-only, by using the +R switch.
autoexec.bat	A foundational boot file used to boot a computer correctly.
CD ROM driver	Copy over CD ROM driver if available.
chkdsk.exe	Checks disk for errors, makes minor repairs, and displays information about the disk. Updated DOS users may use scandisk instead.
config.sys	A foundational boot file used to boot a computer correctly.
edit.com	Edit allows a user to view, create, and/or modify computer files such as autoexec.bat or config.sys.
fdisk.exe	Remove master boot record viruses from the hard drive with FDISK /MBR, or repartition drives. Use this program with caution!
format.com	Formats disks as desired.
MEM	MEM verifies normal memory setup on computer when compared against known "normal" memory settings. Abnormal readings may indicate an infection.
MSD	A diagnostic utility that enables users to view configurations on a computer, helping in some troubleshooting scenarios.
uninstal.exe	Uninstall programs installed on the computer.
unformat.exe	DOS 5.0 or later may use UNFORMAT /L /PARTN to verify normal configurations for partitions on a drive.
scandisk.exe	Scans and corrects disks for basic errors.
scandisk.ini	Initializes the scandisk.exe program. Copy over with Scandisk.
sys.com	Overwrites DOS partition of an infected hard drive with SYS C: command.

Good Times Virus Hoax FAQ

The Good Times e-mail virus is a hoax! If anyone repeats the hoax, please show them the FAQ.

G o o d T i m e s V i r u s H o a x

F r e q u e n t l y A s k e d Q u e s t i o n s

by Les Jones
macfaq@aol.com
lesjones@usit.net
February 6, 1996

This information may be freely reproduced in any medium, as long as the information is unmodified.

February 6, 1995 Update

The Good Times virus hoax keeps on going. I receive almost daily reports of hoax activity. I'm reposting the FAQ to relevant newsgroups, and I've set up my own Web pages:

- http://www.usit.net/public/lesjones/goodtimes.html
- http://www.usit.net/public/lesjones/gtminifaq.html

- http://users.aol.com/macfaq/goodtimes.html
- http://users.aol.com/macfaq/gtminifaq.html

The FAQ has been updated with current URLs and a new section discussing the Word macro virus.

A call to educators and translators

If you teach classes or write books about the Internet, I encourage to educate people about Good Times. The Good Times myth is not going away anytime soon, so we should start including it in Internet curriculum now. The FAQ is free for redistribution in any medium, so feel free to integrate it into any class materials or published works.

Good Times has spread to many countries, and has been translated into many languages. If you are bilingual, you can help debunk Good Times by translating the FAQ into another language. If you do translate the FAQ, please let me know the URL so I can include it in the FAQ.

Is the Good Times e-mail virus a hoax?

Yes. It was a hoax in November of 1994, and it's still a hoax in February of 1996.

America Online, government computer security agencies, and makers of antivirus software have declared Good Times a hoax. See Online References at the end of the FAQ.

Since the hoax began in November of 1994, no copy of the alleged virus has ever been found, nor has there been a single verified case of a viral attack.

Why should I believe the FAQ instead of the hoax?

Unlike the warnings that have been passed around, the FAQ is signed and dated. I've included my e-mail address, and the e-mail addresses of contributors, for verification. I've also provided online references at the end of the FAQ so that you can confirm this information for yourself. I'm new to the Internet.

What is the Good Times virus hoax?

The story is that a virus called Good Times is being carried by e-mail. Just reading a message with "Good Times" in the subject line will erase your hard drive, or even destroy your computer's processor. Needless to say, it's a hoax, but a lot of people believed it.

The original message ended with instructions to "Forward this to all your friends," and many people did just that. Warnings about Good Times have been widely distributed on mailing lists, Usenet newsgroups, and message boards.

The original hoax started in early December of 1994. It sprang up again in March of 1995. In mid-April, a new version of the hoax that mentioned an FCC report began circulating. Worried that Good Times would never go away, I decided to write the FAQ. These worries proved valid when the hoax began popping up again in October of 1995.

What is the effect of the hoax?

For those who already know it's a hoax, it's a nuisance to read the repeated warnings. For people who don't know any better, it causes needless concern and lost productivity.

The virus hoax infects mailing lists, bulletin boards, and Usenet newsgroups. Worried system administrators needlessly worry their employees by posting dire warnings. The hoax is not limited to the United States. It has appeared in several English-speaking and non-English-speaking countries. One reader sent me an English transcription of a radio broadcast in Malta.

Adam J. Kightley (adamjk@cogs.susx.ac.uk) said, "The cases of 'infection' I came across all tended to result from the message getting into the hands of senior noncomputing personnel. Those with the ability and authority to spread it widely, without the knowledge to spot its nonsensical content."

Some of the companies that have reportedly fallen for the hoax include AT&T, CitiBank, NBC, Hughes Aircraft, Microsoft, Texas Instruments, and dozens or hundreds of others. There have been outbreaks at numerous colleges.

The U.S. government has not been immune. Some of the government agencies that have reportedly fallen victim to the hoax include the Department of Defense, the FCC, NASA, the USDA, U.S. Census Bureau, and various national labs. I've confirmed outbreaks at the Department of Health and Human Services, though they had the good sense to question the hoax, and ask for more information on Usenet, before passing the hoax along to their employees.

The virus hoax has occasionally escaped into the popular media. ez018982@betty.ucdavis.edu reports that on April 4, 1995, during the Tom Sullivan show on KFBK 1530 AM radio in Sacramento, California, a police officer warned listeners not to read e-mail labeled "Good Times," and to report the sender to the police. Other radio stations, including Australia's ABC radio, have also spread the hoax.

There are scattered reports of the virus spreading via Faxnet, that low-tech network of secretaries and bored knowledge workers that traffics in cartoons and dumb-blonde jokes.

What was the CIAC bulletin?

On December 6, 1994, the U.S. Department of Energy's CIAC (Computer Incident Advisory Capability) issued a bulletin declaring the Good Times virus a hoax and an urban legend. The bulletin was widely quoted as an antidote to the hoax. The original document can be found at the address in Online References at the end of the FAQ. Note that the document went through several minor revisions, with 94-04c of December 8 being the most recent.

Like all quoted material in the FAQ, it includes the original spelling and punctuation. Because some of the lines in the CIAC report are rather long, they will appear broken.

> THE "Good Times" VIRUS IS AN URBAN LEGEND
> In the early part of December, CIAC started to receive information requests about a supposed "virus" which could be contracted via America OnLine, simply by reading a message.
>
> _____
>
> Here is some important information. Beware of a file called Goodtimes.
> Happy Chanukah everyone, and be careful out there. There is a virus on America Online being sent by E-Mail. If you get anything called "Good Times", DON'T read it or download it. It is a virus that will erase your hard drive. Forward this to all your friends. It may help them a lot.
>
> _____
>
> THIS IS A HOAX. Upon investigation, CIAC has determined that this message originated from both a user of America Online and a student at a university at approximately the same time, and it was meant to be a hoax.
> CIAC has also seen other variations of this hoax, the main one is that any electronic mail message with the subject line of "xxx-1" will infect your computer.
> This rumor has been spreading very widely. This spread is due mainly to the fact that many people have seen a message with "Good Times" in the header. They delete the message without reading it, thus believing that they have saved themselves from being attacked. These first-hand reports give a false sense of credibility to the alert message.
> There has been one confirmation of a person who received a message with "xxx-1" in the header, but an empty message body. Then, (in a panic, because he had

heard the alert), he checked his PC for viruses (the first time he checked his machine in months) and found a preexisting virus on his machine. He incorrectly came to the conclusion that the E-mail message gave him the virus (this particular virus could *not possibly* have spread via an E-mail message). This person then spread his alert.

As of this date, there are no known viruses which can infect merely through reading a mail message. For a virus to spread some program must be executed. Reading a mail message does not execute the mail message. Yes, Trojans have been found as executable attachments to mail messages, the most notorious being the IBM VM Christmas Card Trojan of 1987, also the TERM MODULE Worm (reference CIAC Bulletin B-7) and the GAME2 MODULE Worm (CIAC Bulletin B-12). But this is not the case for this particular "virus" alert.

If you encounter this message being distributed on any mailing lists, simply ignore it or send a follow-up message stating that this is a false rumor.

Karyn Pichnarczyk
CIAC Team
ciac@llnl.gov

Note: Karyn is now with Cisco. Her new e-mail address is karyn@cisco.com.

The CIAC report was wrong when it stated that the hoax was started by "a user of America Online and a student at a university." See "Who started the hoax."

What's the first version of the warning (FYI)?

I have an early version of the hoax that dates back to November 15, 1994, when it was posted to the TECH-LAW mailing list. This is currently the earliest known example of Good Times. See also "When did the hoax start?"

FYI, a file, going under the name "Good Times" is being sent to some Internet users who subscribe to on-line services (Compuserve, Prodigy and America On Line). If you should receive this file, do not download it! Delete it immediately. I understand that there is a virus included in that file, which if downloaded to your personal computer, will ruin all of your files.

One person remembers seeing Good Times as far back as April or May of 1994, but there is no supporting evidence for that claim. For now, the FYI message qualifies as the earliest prototype of Good Times.

What did the first major warning (Happy Chanukah) say?

This is the canonical Happy Chanukah message as I received it on December 2, 1994, and as it was quoted in the CIAC report, though it's not the earliest message. This message was largely responsible for sparking the December Good Times panic.

> Here is some important information. Beware of a file called Goodtimes.
> Happy Chanukah everyone, and be careful out there. There is a virus on America Online being sent by E-Mail. If you get anything called "Good Times", DON'T read it or download it. It is a virus that will erase your hard drive. Forward this to all your friends. It may help them a lot.

What's the other major warning (ASCII)?

The "happy Chanukah" greeting in the original message dates it, so more recent hoax eruptions have used a different message. The one below can be identified because it claims that simply loading Good Times into the computer's ASCII buffer can activate the virus, so I call it ASCII.

Karyn Pichnarczyk (karyn@cisco.com) remembers the ASCII message from the original hoax in December of 1994, though I never saw it. Mikko Hypponen (Mikko.Hypponen@datafellows.fi) sent me a copy of this warning that dates back to December 2, 1994. The Infinite Loop variety of ASCII is now the basis for the most common warnings.

Thought you might like to know...

Apparently , a new computer virus has been engineered by a user of America Online that is unparalleled in its destructive capability. Other, more well-known viruses such as Stoned, Airwolf, and Michaelangelo pale in comparison to the prospects of this newest creation by a warped mentality.

What makes this virus so terrifying is the fact that no program needs to be exchanged for a new computer to be infected. It can be spread through the existing e-mail systems of the InterNet.

Luckily, there is one sure means of detecting what is now known as the "Good Times" virus. It always travels to new computers the same way—in a text e-mail message with the subject line reading simply "Good Times". Avoiding infection is easy once the file has been received—not reading it. The act of loading the file into the mail server's ASCII buffer causes the "Good Times" mainline program to initialize and execute.

The program is highly intelligent—it will send copies of itself to everyone whose e-mail address is contained in a received-mail file or a sent-mail file, if it can find one. It will then proceed to trash the computer it is running on.

The bottom line here is—if you receive a file with the subject line "Good TImes", delete it immediately! Do not read it! Rest assured that whoever's name was on the "From:" line was surely struck by the virus. Warn your friends and local system users of this newest threat to the InterNet! It could save them a lot of time and money.

What's the popular variation on ASCII (FCC or Infinite Loop)?

You rarely see the pure ASCII version any more. One common variation mentions an FCC memo, and claims that Good Times can destroy a computer's processor by placing the processor in an "nth-complexity infinite binary loop," which is a fancy-sounding bit of science fiction. This is by far the most common version nowadays, and consists of ASCII with the following additional material:

> The FCC released a warning last Wednesday concerning a matter of major importance to any regular user of the InterNet. Apparently, a new computer virus has been engineered by a user of America Online that is unparalleled in its destructive capability. Other, more well-known viruses such as Stoned, Airwolf, and Michaelangelo pale in comparison to the prospects of this newest creation by a warped mentality.
>
> What makes this virus so terrifying, said the FCC, is the fact that no program needs to be exchanged for a new computer to be infected. It can be spread through the existing e-mail systems of the InterNet. Once a computer is infected, one of several things can happen. If the computer contains a hard drive, that will most likely be destroyed. If the program is not stopped, the computer's processor will be placed in an nth-complexity infinite binary loop—which can severely damage the processor if left running that way too long. Unfortunately, most novice computer users will not realize what is happening until it is far too late.

Exactly when did the hoax start?

I thought I knew, but new evidence has come to light. In the original FAQ, I wrote the following paragraphs:

> December 2, 1994 is often quoted as the beginning of the hoax, but some of the AOL forward message headers in the copy I received put the date at December 1. One non-AOL header is dated November 29, though that date could easily have been forged.
>
> Also, notice the text of the original message as it was sent to me, and quoted in the CIAC report:
>
> Here is some important information. Beware of a file called Goodtimes. Happy Chanukah everyone, and be careful out there. There is a virus on America Online

being sent by E-Mail. If you get anything called "Good Times", DON'T read it or download it. It is a virus that will erase your hard drive. Forward this to all your friends. It may help them a lot.

The first paragraph suggests that someone was forwarding the information in the second paragraph. A seasonal greeting like "Happy Chanukah" is almost never placed in the second paragraph of a letter, suggesting even more strongly that this message was repeating information from someone else.

After reading the FAQ, several people reported earlier instances of the hoax. On November 15, 1994, Rich Lavoie (lavoie@cwt.com) posted it to the TECH-LAW mailing list. Rodney Knight (r.j.knight@rl.ac.uk) saw that message on a newsgroup, and forwarded the warning to the POSTCARD mailing list. November 15 is currently the earliest confirmed sighting.

Anthony Altieri (magneto@epix.net) and many others recollected the hoax as far back as April or May of 1994, but that recollection is so far unsubstantiated by any evidence.

Who started the hoax?

We don't know who started the hoax. You'll meet people who think they know who started it, or where it started. They are misinformed. Show them the FAQ. I've seen some people claim that the hoaxsters were arrested and convicted. This is incorrect.

The CIAC report stated that the hoax was started by "a user of America Online and a student at a university." I asked Karyn Pichnarczyk about that. During the December outbreak of Happy Chanukah, several people tried to trace the hoax by following message headers. When America Online traced headers, they stopped at an AOL account. When Nathan Gilliatt (gilliatt@ac.duke.edu) traced headers in different messages, the messages seemed to stop at Swarthmore College.

Karyn said she didn't know who to believe, so she said that the virus was started by "a user of America Online and a student at a university." We now know that "Happy Chanukah" wasn't the original message, so tracing headers was a futile attempt to trace the origin of the hoax.

What theories do we have about the hoax's origins?

Asking who started the hoax assumes that someone consciously started the hoax. It's remotely possible that Good Times is a highly distorted report of some real or semi-real event. After being told and retold, the story became the Good Times hoax as we know it. The Telephone Game gone mad. The problem with this theory is that it's probably impossible to prove.

AOL postmaster David O'Donnell (PMDAtropos@aol.com) has another theory about the origins of the hoax. David says that there was once a Good Times chain letter going around. To stop the chain letter, David's theory goes, someone claimed that the chain letter contained a virus, and warned people to delete any e-mail with "Good Times" in the subject line. Alan Braggins (armb@setanta.demon.co.uk) and others recall seeing the chain letter prior to the virus hoax.

If anyone saved those old messages, I'd love to see one. So far, no one has been able to produce any of the Good Luck messages. Unlike paper, the Internet and Usenet are programmed to purge old data on a regular basis in the name of disk-space efficiency.

Is an e-mail virus possible?

The short answer is no, not the way Good Times was described.

The long answer is that this is a difficult question that's open to nit-picking. Keep three things in mind when considering the question:

- A virus is operating system–specific. DOS viruses don't affect Macintoshes, and vice versa. That greatly limits the destructive power of viruses. (And notice that none of the Good Times warnings mentions which types of computers are affected. That omission set off many people's hoax detectors.) For an exception, see "What about the Word macro virus?" below.

- A virus, by definition, can't exist by itself. It must infect an executable program. To transmit a virus by e-mail, someone would have to infect a file and attach the file to the e-mail message. To activate the virus, you would have to download and decode the file attachment, then run the infected program. In that situation, the e-mail message is just a carrier for an infected file, just like a floppy disk carrying an infected file.

- Some of the situations that people have dreamed up involve Trojan horses rather than viruses. A virus can only exist inside another program, which then automatically infects other programs. A Trojan horse is a program that pretends to do something useful, but instead does something nefarious. Trojans aren't infectious, so they're much less common and much less destructive than viruses.

There are some e-mail programs that can be set to automatically download a file attachment, decode it, and execute the file attachment. If you use such a program, you would be well advised to disable the option to automatically execute file attachments.

You should, of course, be wary of any file attachments a stranger sends you. At the least, you should check such file attachments for viruses before running them.

What about the Word macro virus?

After I posted the FAQ to Usenet in October of 1995, many people wrote to mention the Word macro virus, which had recently stepped into the light. Sometimes known as the Winword.concept virus or the Word prank macro virus, it breaks the rule that viruses are operating system-specific by infecting both Macs and PCs running several different operating systems. Breaking another rule, it infects documents instead of programs.

Why can the Word macro virus affect several operating systems?

When programmers write code, they typically write the source code in a text file. The source code is then run through a compiler, which converts the source code into instructions that can be understood by a certain type of operating system. That's why most programs (including most viruses) can only run under one type of operating system. The resulting program is variously called a binary, application, or executable, and can function by itself.

Programmers can also run the source code through an interpreter, which executes the code line by line, but does not produce an executable program. The Word macro virus is an example of an interpreted program. The interpreter in this case is the Word Basic macro facility that's part of Word 6.0 for Windows, Word for Windows 95, Word for Windows NT, and Word 6.0 for Macintosh. The same source code (the macro virus) runs on four different operating systems because the interpreter (Word Basic) is available on all four operating systems. (I'll be generous and call Windows 3.1 an operating system.)

What does the Word macro virus do?

This text is excerpted from M. David Stone's excellent article in the February, 1996, issue of *PC Magazine:*

> An infected document is actually a template masquerading as a document. The virus manages this trick because although uses a .DOT extension by default for

templates, it doesn't require that .DOT extension. And a template, by any name, can store macros. The key to the Winword.concept virus is an AutoOpen macro, which runs each time you open the document. When you open an infected document, the virus modifies the Normal template, Normal.dot, which Word keeps loaded at all times—even when you're using another template. Once infected, Normal.dot will infect any documents you save with the Save As command. And since Word calls on the Save As command every time you save a new document, that means every new document you create will be infected.

The good news about the Winword.concept virus is that, at least in its original form, it's only annoying, not harmful. (The virus contains the comment "That's enough to prove my point. Obviously the anonymous author wanted to show that a virus could be transmitted via a macro, but didn't feel the need to be destructive about it.) The bad news is that the virus was unleashed on the world in unencrypted form. That means that anyone who gets a hold if it and understands just a little bit of Word Basic can modify it to do serious harm—like erasing files from your hard disk. (I won't go into specifics for obvious reasons.)

For more information, see:
http://www.icubed.com/virus/wordviru.txt

How can I protect myself?

For information and a free set of tools to inoculate Word against the macro virus, see Microsoft's web page at

http://www.microsoft.com/msoffice/freestuf/msword/download/mvtool/mvtool2.htm

How can I protect myself from viruses in general?

Use a virus checker regularly. Freeware, shareware, and commercial antivirus programs are widely available. Which program you use isn't as important as how often you use it. Most people get into trouble because they never bother to check their computer for viruses.

Most viruses spread through floppy disks, so isolating yourself from online services and the Internet will not protect you from viruses. In fact, you're probably safer if you're online, simply because you'll have access to antiviral software and information.

Q. Where can I find antiviral information on the Internet?

A. *Usenet newsgroups*
comp.virus—the Usenet gateway for VIRUS-L (below)

A. *Mailing lists*
VIRUS-L is a moderated list for discussions of viruses and antiviral products. To subscribe, send e-mail to listserv@lehigh.edu. In the body of the message, include the line "sub virus-l your-real-name" (without the quotes).

A. *FTP sites*
cert.org in pub/virus-l/docs/
Contains information about viruses and antivirus products, with pointers to other FTP sites.

A. *World Wide Web*
http://www.singnet.com.sg/staff/lorna/Virus
(Note: the V must be capitalized!)
Antivirus Resources, Antivirus Software
http://www.primenet.com/%7Emwest/av.htm
The Virus Information Page
http://www.towson.edu/%7Ejack/virus/virus.html
Antivirus Center
http://www.antivirus.com/
Monkey Shines Virus Web Page
http://www.sasknet.com/%7Ebronm/
How to Handle a Virus Attack
http://www.primenet.com/%7Emwest/vir-atk.htm
Data Fellow's Computer Virus Descriptions
http://www.datafellows.fi/vir-desc.htm
Computer Virus Jokes

http://www.usmcs.maine.edu/%7Elaferrie/humor/
compvir.html

Q. Was the hoax a sort of virus itself?

A. Yes, but it wasn't a computer virus. It was more
like a social virus or a thought virus.

When someone on alt.folklore.urban asked if the
virus was for real, Clay Shirky (clays@panix.com)
answered: "Its for real. Its an opportunistic self-repli-
cating e-mail virus which tricks its host into replicating it, sometimes adding as many as 200,000 copies at
a go. It works by finding hosts with defective parsing
apparatus which prevents them from understanding
that a piece of e-mail which says there is an e-mail
virus and then asking them to remail the message to
all their friends is the virus itself."

Shirky eloquently described what a lot of people
were thinking. So what is a virus? To a biologist, a
virus is a snippet of genetic material that must infect
a host organism to survive and reproduce. To be contagious, a virus usually carries instructions that cause
the host to engage in certain pathological activities
(such as sneezing and coughing) that spread the infection to other organisms.

To a computer programmer, a virus is a snippet of
computer code that must infect a host program to
spread. To be contagious, a computer virus usually
causes the host program to engage in certain pathological activities that spread the infection to other
programs.

From this perspective, it's easy to see the Good
Times hoax as a sort of thought virus. To be contagious, a thought virus causes the host to engage in certain pathological activities that spread the infection.

In the case of Good Times, the original strain (Happy
Chanukah) explicitly told people to "forward this to all
your friends." The other major viral strain (infinite
loop) encourages people to "Please be careful and for-

ward this mail to anyone you care about," and "Warn your friends and local system users of this newest threat to the InterNet!"

Likewise, the stories of an FCC modem tax encourage people to tell their friends and post the warning on other BBSes. David Rhodes' Make Money Fast scam instructs people to re-post the message to as many as ten bulletin boards.

In *The Selfish Gene* (1976, University of Oxford Press), Oxford evolutionary biologist Richard Dawkins extends the principles in his book from biology to human culture. To make the transition, Dawkins proposes a cultural replicator analogous to genes. He calls these replicators "memes."

Examples of memes are tunes, ideas, catch-phrases, clothes fashions, ways of making pots or of building arches. Just as genes propagate themselves in the gene pool by leaping from body to body via sperm or eggs, so memes propagate themselves in the meme pool by leaping from brain to brain via a process which, in the broad sense, can be called imitation....As my colleague N. K. Humphrey neatly summed up an earlier draft of this section: "...memes should be regarded as living structures, not just metaphorically, but technically. When you plant a fertile meme in my mind you literally parasitize my brain, turning it into a vehicle for the meme's propagation in just the way that a virus may parasitize the genetic mechanism of a host cell."

Amazingly, when I read alt.folklore.computers looking for research material, two people had already mentioned Dawkins' memes. One of them referred to an article in the April 8, 1995 *New Scientist* about something called the Meme Research Group. (The article erroneously stated that the group is at the University of California, San Francisco. In fact, they are at Simon Fraser University in British Columbia.)

The Meme Research Group is collecting chain letters to analyze them. The more copies they get, the more information they have to analyze. Send those unwanted chain letters to meme@scottlabsgi.chem.sfu.ca.

I am not a memeticist, and a real memeticist might take umbrage at my explanation of the concept. To learn more, visit the alt.memetics newsgroup on Usenet, and especially the alt.memetics home page on the World Wide Web (http://www.xs4all.nl/~hingh/alt.memetics/). Though we've talked about memes in terms of viruses (a common analogy), the concept of a meme is neither good nor bad. The idea of "Do unto others as you would have them do unto you" is as much a meme as the Good Times hoax.

What's the best way to control a thought virus?

Create a countervirus like this one as an antidote. To make the countervirus contagious, include instructions such as, "The Good Times e-mail virus is a hoax. If anyone repeats the hoax, please show them the FAQ."

What are some other hoaxes and urban legends on the Internet?

The FCC Modem Tax

Every so often someone posts a dire warning that the FCC is considering a tax on modems and online services. The warning encourages you to tell your friends so they can take political action. It's a hoax. It's been going on for the five years I've been online, and probably much longer. If you'll notice, the warnings don't include a date or a bill number.

Make Money Fast

If you haven't seen a Make Money Fast message, call your local anthropology department. They might be interested in studying you. Devised by David Rhodes in 1987 or 1988, Make Money Fast (sometimes distributed on BBSes as a file called fastcash.txt) is an electronic version of a chain letter pyramid scheme. You're supposed to send money to the ten people on the list, then add your name to the list and repost the chain letter, committing federal wire fraud in the process. Posting a Make Money Fast message is one sure way to lose your Internet account. (Information from the Make Money Fast FAQ by ewl@panix.com.)

Craig Shergold needs your get well cards

Craig Shergold is a UK resident who was dying of cancer. He wanted to get in the *Guinness Book of World Records* for having received the most get well cards. When people heard of the poor boy's wish, they began sending him postcards. And they kept sending him postcards, and never stopped. Shergold is now in full remission. He was listed in the *Guinness Book of World Records* in 1991. He really does not want your postcards any more, and neither does his hometown post office.

These are just the urban legends that you're likely to encounter on the Internet. There are many more in real life that you probably believe. I won't give them away, but here are some clues: peanut butter, Neiman Marcus/Mrs. Fields, Rod Stewart, and the Newlywed Game. For more information, read the alt.folklore.urban FAQ, listed in Online References at the end of the FAQ.

Online References (including this FAQ)

CIAC Notes 94-05, 95-09, and especially 94-04

http://ciac.llnl.gov/ciac/notes/Notes04c.shtml
http://ciac.llnl.gov/ciac/notes/Notes05d.shtml
http://ciac.llnl.gov/ciac/notes/Notes09.shtml
Data Fellows' description of Good Times
http://www.datafellows.fi/v-descs/goodtime.htm
Australian Cert Note

ftp://ftp.auscert.org.au/pub/auscert/advisory/AL-
95.02.virus.hoax.returns

alt.folklore.urban FAQ

Available via FTP from cathouse.org in the
/pub/cathouse/urban.legends/AFU.faq directory.
Also available on the World Wide Web at
http://cathouse.org/UrbanLegends/AFUFAQ/

The Good Times Virus Hoax FAQ and Mini FAQ

The mini FAQ is a greatly simplified version of this
FAQ. At two pages, it's short enough for message
boards, faxes, mailing lists, and people with short
attention spans.

http://www.usit.net/public/lesjones/goodtimes.html
http://www.usit.net/public/lesjones/gtminifaq.html
http://users.aol.com/macfaq/goodtimes.html
http://users.aol.com/macfaq/gtminifaq.html
Via FTP:
ftp://usit.net/pub/lesjones/good-times-virus-
hoax-faq.txt
ftp://usit.net/pub/lesjones/good-times-virus-hoax-
mini-faq.txt
ftp://users.aol.com/macfaq/good-times-virus-hoax-
faq.txt
ftp://users.aol.com/macfaq/good-times-virus-hoax-
mini-faq.txt
On America Online:
In the file libraries at keyword VIRUS.

Identifying Hoaxes Lesson Plan

From About.com at http://antivirus.about.com, use this lesson plan to help students better understand hoaxes and viruses.

Preparation

- Time varies—30 minutes to several days. Present the lesson with traditional lecture style for a 15- to 30-minute overview of hoaxes.

- Print out sample hoaxes from http://antivirus.about.com/library/blenhoax.htm.

- Print out real warnings from company memoranda or online sources such as CIAC.

- Organize groups based upon temperament, ability levels, gender, etc.

Delivery

Start the class by handing out several hoax and authentic messages.

- Ask students to read each carefully, writing down any thoughts they may have, on each paper, while reading the message.

- Entertain class discussion and comments regarding all messages. Develop feedback regarding legitimacy and concerns of hoaxes. Ask open-ended questions helping students to better understand hoaxes, such as "Are there any statements that you believe to be untrue?"

- Ask the class, "How can you tell the difference between a hoax and an authentic message/e-mail?" After entertaining a brief classroom discussion, break into groups.

Ask each group to identify each message as either hoax or authentic, stating why.

- Circulate around the room checking on the progress and cooperative skills of each group. Facilitate as necessary.

- Note student feedback and comments within groups and question/clarify to help facilitate deeper discussion and considerations. Example, "I see that you have identified this statement as unbelievable—is there a way you can verify the accuracy of the statement with an expert in the field?; How could you find out more about the accuracy of this statement?"

Ask each group to quickly share their determinations and support for each.

- Keep track of determinations on a chalkboard/overhead to tally results for each sample analyzed. For example, sample one may be identified as "hoax" by 3 groups and as "authentic" by 1 group.

- Manage the class carefully to avoid discussion or dispute during this sharing period.

Ask each group to quickly review class determinations and make any changes to their own if desired.

- Circulate around the classroom and help facilitate the reasoning process using the new data of class determinations for each group. Prompt students to support their answers with data and logic instead of peer pressure (popular vote).

- Ask each group to identify any changes desired and note on board/overhead.
- Briefly discuss changes made, if any, and ask why the changes were made.

Review each sample, in detail, facilitating feedback from the entire class as a group.

- Allow for plenty of discussion, as time permits.
- Facilitate the exploration of the legitimacy of various statements/claims as they are questioned by the group.
- Ask students how they might verify the legitimacy of a message. Write answers on the board/overhead.

Identify hoax and authentic messages.

- If time permits, as homework or an extension of the instruction, have students verify the legitimacy of each message. Ideally, one sample is assigned to each student. Then, groups, based upon sample assignment, collect and analyze their results the follow day(s) to discuss and identify the sample as hoax or authentic. Also, valuable resources used in research may also be identified by each group/class.
- If little time remains, simply go through the list and identify each sample as hoax or authentic, pointing out major features aiding in the identification of the message.
- Make the class fun by giving out small rewards for correct answers, 100 percent correct labeling, etc.

Identify official sources of information and discuss.

- Individually, or as a group, have students identify official sources for additional information. If development of official resources is an important part of instruction develop a reward system for finding the most official links, including manufacturers of antivirus software, CIAC, and other leading antivirus sites such as About.com Antivirus Software.

- Discuss as a class the values of each site identified and organize a set of support materials from class-generated information.

- Disseminate materials and/or training to other classes, teachers, or organizations to better support the authentic value of material created by the class. For example, create a Web site with class results, links, and information about hoaxes.

- Follow up instruction by providing the class with several messages not included in previous discussions.

- Have each class member read, research, and identify each sample as hoax or authentic. Assemble students in groups to discuss their answers, and then discuss as a class.

- Another great extension of this lesson is to implement a support group, managed by students/employees, to handle incoming messages. For example, if a new message is received in a school, students may do the research and qualify the accuracy of the report with the lead instructor for the project. Results may be posted online or within the organization using traditional methods of communication.

Index

About the Author

Ken Dunham, renowned anti-virus professional, reveals various troubleshooting scenarios, making this practical reference invaluable for all computer professionals and technicians.